Mountain Berries & Desert Spice

SUMAYYA USMANI

Mountain Berries & Desert Spice

SWEET INSPIRATION FROM THE
HUNZA VALLEY TO THE ARABIAN SEA

SUMAYYA USMANI

FOOD PHOTOGRAPHY BY JOANNA YEE

FRANCES
LINCOLN

Frances Lincoln Limited
A Subsidiary of Quarto Publishing Group UK
74–77 White Lion Street
London N1 9PF

Mountain Berries & Desert Spice
Copyright © Frances Lincoln 2017
Text copyright © Sumayya Usmani 2017
Food photography copyright © Joanna Yee
Design: Sarah Allberrey
Commissioning editor: Zena Alkayat

Travel photography copyright © as listed on p182

A catalogue record for this book is available from the British Library

ISBN 978-0-7112-3852-7

Printed and bound in China

9 8 7 6 5 4 3 2 1

Quarto is the authority on a wide range of topics.

Quarto educates, entertains and enriches the
lives of our readers – enthusiasts and lovers of
hands-on living.

www.QuartoKnows.com

This book is dedicated to those I love — may these flavours always be part of your lives — and to the people of my homeland, who share the spiced sweetness of our desserts with joy.

Contents

Journey through a land of sweetness and spice   9

Childhood sweets in a new home   17

Key ingredients and techniques   21

Sour morning berries   29
Rising to mouth-watering spice

Sugar almonds and buffalo milk   51
The sweetness of diversity

Kites, kingdoms and cardamom samosas   73
Flavours from Lahore and the Mughal Empire

Through mulberry valleys   95
Summer fruits in harsh winters

A saffron blaze   117
Following the spice caravans

Festive spice and roses   139
Celebratory sweets

Chilli mangoes and ocean breeze   161
The sweetness of homecoming

Acknowledgements   182

Index   186

Journey through a land of sweetness and spice

Pakistan has long been a passageway for communities and cultures, and a confluence of diverse influences. A rich and turbulent history has seen the country swept through by Mongol invaders and Alexander the Great's armies, ruled by Mughal emperors and affected by British colonialism. Over hundreds and thousands of years, Pakistan has inherited many traditions and its past has left an indelible mark on the contemporary culture and cooking of its people. The country's culinary fabric has also been touched by its geographic borders with Afghanistan, Iran and Central Asia, and enhanced by Muslim emigrants from India. It is home to a multitude of ethnicities, which each brings its own recipes and heritage.

But Pakistan is not only a land of varied people – it is one of varied climate and terrain, and therefore produce. Icy soaring mountains and arid deserts meet fertile plains and deep valleys: dramatic and beautiful, this landscape is capable of supporting the cultivation of a broad natural larder from sweet berries to fiery spice.

Pakistan's bounty is captivating, plentiful and exotic, and the way in which different people and communities cook both savoury and sweet food in the country is greatly dependent on the produce available to them across this changing and vast landscape. But there is one unifying adoration that reigns supreme across the country, and that is the people's love for desserts, confection, fruit and nuts – no Pakistani table is ever without this celebration of sweetness.

The country's northern areas are blessed with fruits such as pomegranates, mulberries and cherries, as well as nuts such as pistachios, walnuts and pine nuts, which all grow easily. In the rugged mountains and valleys of Chitral, Kalash, Gilgit and Hunza, hot milk is flavoured with local honey, and the breeze carries with it the sweet scent of apricots. In the warmer months, these are dried on the foothills, and the dried fruit is then served with fresh cheese to end a meal or greet a guest.

In the southern part of the country, sweets are more spiced and floral. In the dry majestic deserts of Balochistan, which borders Iran, spices such as saffron, cardamom and pepper are grown and used abundantly. Sweets are simple and made using local wheat and dates which have been dried for the harsh winters ahead. Here, saffron- and cardamom-infused milk, as well as rice puddings and buffalo milk sweetmeats, are popular.

A real melting pot of flavours can be found on the streets of my home town Karachi in the southern region of Sindh. Here, diverse sweets reflect the various communities, as well as influences from Mumbai, east Punjab and Hyderabad, and local Sindhi cuisine. Sindh's summer fields are amber with ripe sugar cane, and its lush trees are heavy with pink guavas and honey mangoes, while winter brings the sweetest red carrots. Sweetmeat shops are packed with colourful handmade morsels sold by the kilo, made with raw sugar and spices.

Flavours differ in Lahore – a city in the east which is known as Pakistan's food captial. Here, there is a celebration of the bounty of the fertile lands of Punjab, and sweets might take the form of vegetable halvas, milky rose-scented rice puddings and cardamom- and kewra-infused sweetmeats.

A journey through the sweet flavours of my homeland is diverse, much like its history and land. Sweets and desserts vary in grandeur depending on the occasion. Decadent desserts are a fundemental part of celebrations and festivities, but on a daily basis mithai are a staple. Mithai simply means sweetmeats, and they can be a humble afternoon tea treat or a special gift to a loved one. To a Pakistani, sharing and giving mithai comes easily. This can be a present to show appreciation, rejoice on a happy occasion, or merely an act of kindness to bring a smile to someone's face.

Pakistani people have an adoration of 'muh meetha karna' (sweetening one's mouth), a lyrical expression that defines the very essence of dessert culture, which is far more than simply concluding a main meal. It's about savouring, sharing and celebrating happiness by indulging in sweetness with your loved ones. Whether it's a dawwat (feast) or a friend coming over for chai, there's always a platter of decadent dessert, perfumed mithai or halvas – this practice reflects the nation's sweet tooth, sense of hospitality and love for sharing joy and sweetness with all.

Many people shy away from making South Asian desserts as they feel that they are complicated to make or perhaps not as important as the savoury dishes. I can assure you that if you stop viewing these desserts as an appendage to a meal, and instead look at them as a fundamental part of our food culture and an indulgence to savour, you will soon find yourself under the spell of the exotic flavours, historical romance and comfort of Pakistani desserts.

Pakistan

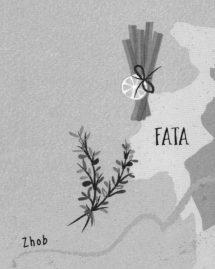

AFGHANISTAN

FATA

Zhob

● Quetta

SAFFRON

BALOCHISTAN

IRAN

Rakkshan

Mashkal

SINDH

Dasht

Gawadar
●

Indus

● Karachi

ARABIAN SEA

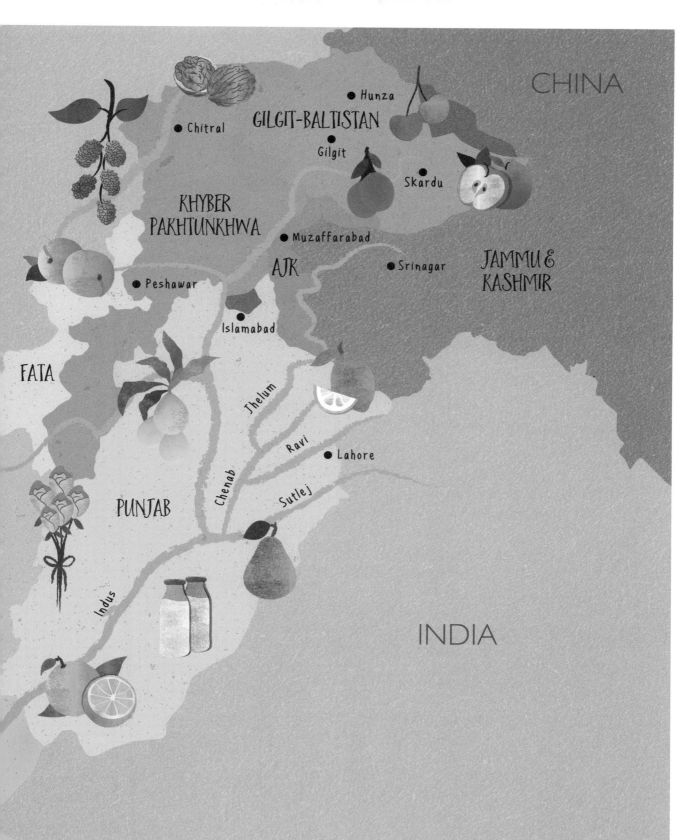

CHINA

Hunza

Chitral

GILGIT-BALTISTAN

Gilgit

Skardu

KHYBER
PAKHTUNKHWA

Muzaffarabad

AJK

Srinagar

JAMMU &
KASHMIR

Peshawar

Islamabad

FATA

Jhelum

Ravi

Lahore

Chenab

Sutlej

PUNJAB

Indus

INDIA

Childhood sweets in a new home

It was my mother who did all of the cooking when I was growing up, and while she made sure there were always desserts, she never had much of a sweet tooth herself, save for one indulgence. Passing by a mithai (sweetmeat) shop, she would stop for a barfi heart – these perfectly shaped sweets made from khoya (milk fudge) were headily infused with rose water and cardamom and would crumble and melt in the mouth.

Much like a child's weekly trip to the sweetie shop in the West, in Pakistan I would get pocket money to buy my favourite mithais. A couple of rupees would buy a crumpled greasy brown paper bag filled with either tiny colourful dots of boondi (sweet, fried chickpea flour), a flaky patisa (a ghee- and sugar-packed sweet), or sometimes a sticky, sugary cottage cheese called cham cham, which I would always buy to share with my Nani (maternal grandmother). There is something wonderful about mithai shops: you're greeted with a smile and air that's thick with sugar, cardamom and fudge-like aromas, as well as a multitude of colours, assorted shapes and piles of sugar-soaked saffron doughnuts. It's really quite magical.

My early childhood was spent on the seas with my father who was a merchant navy captain and my earliest memory of making desserts is helping my mother to mix fudge on an electric frying pan in the ship's galley. When we moved back to dry land in 1980, my mother returned to making more traditional desserts, and most special to me was when her kitchen would come alive with the scents of indulgent Eid desserts. She would get up at the crack of dawn and slave away, meticulously making daal ka halva (lentil halva), seviyan (sweet vermicelli) and gajar ka halva (carrot halva) for what seemed like hours. This sensory recollection comes alive today the moment cloves, cardamom

and saffron infuse in a dessert – these transport me to gleeful moments watching my mother make Pakistani sweets, decorating them with thin slivers of pistachios and almonds and brushing them with silver leaf.

I was never taught many of my grandmother's and mother's desserts, but I can cook them from the memory of the flavour and use andaza (estimation and sensory cooking), to recreate the dishes, no matter how simple or complicated. This is the ethos of Pakistani cookery.

Growing up in the UK, my daughter Ayaana's greatest link to her Pakistani heritage are the flavours of my childhood and she's learning the art of andaza. I find her taking interest in making Pakistani seviyan and a halva of any kind. Her understanding for spicing is slowly growing and she helped to create the flavours of the festive truffles on p155.

Many Pakistani desserts can be very sweet (Pakistanis have a very sweet tooth!), so I have adapted the levels of sugar in my recipes and balanced the spices to ensure that they complement local produce available in the West. Of course, if you enjoy them sweeter, add more sugar!

Though some Pakistani dessert recipes may seem challenging, I would urge you not to be deterred from trying to make them. I find the process therapeutic, and the end result is an offering of love and commitment. To this day desserts in my home mean a time for hospitality and 'muh meetha karna' (sweetening the mouth) of those I love. Desserts help me maintain the heart of Pakistani culture in my home away from home.

Key ingredients and techniques

Many recipes in this book feature a key ingredient or one that needs some preparation. Using and creating these base ingredients was something I learnt by andaza (estimation), but I have aimed to describe them and break down some processes into methods you can follow. I have tried to make these as straightforward and modern as possible, but I never steer too far from authenticity.

Sweetness

Gur / jaggery

Many Pakistani desserts and sweets use jaggery, which is natural unrefined sugar cane, date, coconut sap or palm molasses. In Pakistan we mainly use sugar cane jaggery: the flavour is nutty and fudgy, the sweetness is caramel-like and less sweet than white sugar. It is healthier than refined white sugar too, and has health benefits including detoxifying the liver and aiding digestion. It can be bought crushed, in liquid form, or powdered (sold as 'shakar' to be used in tea), but is mostly found in solid blocks. The fresher it is, the crumblier the block is. Most South Asian stores stock jaggery, but a close substitute would be dark brown sugar, muscovado sugar, demerara sugar or panela – but you will need to alter the quantity according to taste. As a child, I loved sucking on chunks of jaggery, and would call it natural fudge!

White sugar

Sugar is an ingredient that Pakistanis would be lost without. It's used in savoury dishes, sweets and drinks across the Subcontinent, making sugar a store cupboard essential. When I was young, we could only buy coarse white sugar: the grains were chunky and it was a treat sneaking a teaspoon of it from the sugar pot. Of course, these days fine sugar is easily available. Pakistanis also use misri (rock sugar), which is composed of relatively large sugar crystals formed by dissolving sugar in water and then leaving it to crystallise over a number of days. Misri is usually used as an after-dinner mouth freshener, or the crystals are stuck on to sticks to be stirred through tea (an adopted Iranian custom), but I find misri adds an interesting sugar crunch to desserts too.

Generally, white sugar (or you can use golden caster sugar) is added to halvas, together with the main ingredient, or it is added as a sugar syrup. The consistency of these syrups is really important. Pakistanis don't usually own a sugar thermometer and all syrups are made to a consistency of 'ek taar' (single thread) or 'do taar' (double thread), and sometimes 'teen taar' (triple thread). The recipe for these is below.

My typical measure is 2 parts sugar to 1 part water and I use an ordinary cup to measure with
In a saucepan, dissolve the sugar in the water over a medium heat and bring to the boil. When it starts to bubble, lower the heat and allow it to simmer. While it's simmering, use the finger press method to determine whether it's ready.

Dip a wooden spoon into the mixture, then carefully touch your finger against the syrup on the spoon – then press your finger against your thumb. As the two pull apart, notice how many threads stretch between your finger and thumb. As soon as the desired thread consistency is reached, take the syrup off the heat.

Single thread syrup is reached at approximately 110°C/230°F–112°C/234°F. It's used for sweets that absorb the syrup, such as Pakistani jalebis (see p78).

Double thread (or soft ball syrup) is reached at approximately 112°C/234°F–116°C/241°F. This is used for making sweets that need sugar to set, such as balushahi curd doughnuts (see p142).

Triple thread syrup creates a hard ball of sugar which can be used to make hard candies or brittles, such as the sesame rewri (see p176). Keep simmering the syrup until it reaches approximately 121°C/250°F–130°C/266°F.

Condensed milk

Condensed milk is sweet and milky. I have placed it under 'sweetness' rather than 'milky' because, for me, it primarily alters sweetness and reduces or eliminates the need to add sugar to a dessert. It also helps thicken puddings and saves time in recipes that might require you to reduce milk.

Sheerni / mulberry syrup

Mulberry syrup is frequently used as a sweetener in the north of Pakistan, where white and black mulberries grow from late spring through to summer. Sheerni is made by simmering one part fresh black mulberries (or dried mulberries) together with one part sugar over a low flame overnight. By morning, what's left is a thick syrup. It's divine on Chitrali rishiki (see p99) and on buttered toast – use sparingly, though, as it is really heady, sweet and intense. You can also buy mulberry syrup in specialist grocery stores and online.

Honey

Honey is produced across Pakistan from Punjab to the Swat district and is popularly added to milk drinks and drizzled over pancakes and on flatbreads for breakfast.

Spice

Saffron

Saffron has an earthy, floral smell in the jar, but when steeped in hot water or hot milk, it releases its real potency. Use sparingly to evoke a hint of Pakistan's sultry summer days.

Green cardamom

Green cardamom is very frequently used in Pakistani desserts. The seeds are removed from the husk and freshly ground, releasing an intense aroma. This mellows when used in cooked, milk-based desserts and is heightened in baking.

Black cardamom

This is not traditionally used in Pakistani desserts, but I love the smoky peaty essence it gives when infused in milk- and rice-based desserts or pancake batters.

Cloves

In Pakistan, cloves are added to most halvas, especially carrot, daal and semolina ones. As opposed to that Christmas scent cloves are associated with in the West, cloves merely bring about a warm, spicy yet mellow flavour in Pakistani desserts, and are usually used in partnership with cardamom and rose water. Use judiciously in order to avoid a bitter flavour in halvas.

Black pepper

Though not used very often in desserts, I think black pepper works well with nuts and jaggery – it's one to play around with, especially if you add it to dessert recipes from northern Pakistan, where pepper is the main spice in many savoury dishes.

Dried ginger

Dried ginger powder has a much stronger ginger hit than the fresh stem. It's found in many drinks and a few regional desserts, but generally used sparingly to add a warming heat.

Nutmeg and mace

These are twin spices. They both add a comforting aroma to milk-based desserts. Nutmeg is much easier to use grated, whereas mace can be used to infuse syrups or milk by slowly boiling. Mace should be used more carefully than nutmeg as it has a greater impact on flavour. Very few Pakistani desserts use this spice, but I love experimenting with it where I can as its floral spicing is very unique.

Rose

Rose is one of the most popular floral flavours in Pakistani desserts. We add this either as rose syrup (Rooh Afza is the most common brand), rose essence or rose water. The aromas of Pakistani desi gulab (a local, red rose variety) are exotic and powerful and they give desserts a regal and festive finish.

Kewra

Kewra is extracted from the pandanus plant and is usually sold as kewra water, or as a stronger extract or essence. You can find these in most Asian shops. The aroma is pungent, but floral. It can appear mellow in sugar syrups or intense when combined with milk. Use sparingly as it is strong and an acquired taste.

Texture

Roasted vermicelli

Vermicelli is durum wheat (semolina)-based fine pasta that has been pre-roasted. This can be found in most Asian stores, especially around the time of Eid, as it is a traditional dessert ingredient. Pre-roasting gives it a nutty flavour, and it soaks up sugar syrups or milk and doubles in size (just like pasta), so be careful how much you use. The texture is crunchy when toasted in butter or ghee and sugar, but it can also be softened in milk or sugar syrup.

Grains

Pakistani desserts are often made from semolina (both coarse and fine), ground and whole basmati rice, channa daal, moong daal, buckwheat and wheatgerm. Pakistani desserts tend to favour grains as they add a nutty flavour, gritty texture and bulk that allows many desserts and sweets to either thicken more quickly (halvas) or bind together well (for sweetmeat-style sweets).

Flours

Many desserts use chickpea flour, rice flour or buckwheat flour. Chickpea flour has a nutty flavour, as well as a soft pliable texture when wet (unlike white flour which can become sticky). Rice flour is gritty and expands when cooking, so it can thicken up sweets or (when used as a dry coating) create a crunch on the outside of fried sweets.

Nuts

Nuts form a big part of Pakistani desserts, either as the main ingredient or a garnish. In the north, trees are laden with walnuts, and there are pine nuts, pistachios and apricots (the kernel is widely used like a nut). In the south, there are almond trees – the raw fruit of which is eaten as well as the nuts.

Milky

Khoya / Pakistani milk fudge

Milk fudge is the closest comparison to khoya – a key base ingredient used in many Pakistani desserts. Khoya is essentially thickened whole milk, cooked down for hours to resemble dulce de leche. The milk is cooked without any added sweetener, but over hours of slow cooking it develops a slight sweetness from the concentration of lactose as it becomes milk solids. Be careful to keep the milk over a low heat and stir frequently to avoid it burning from the bottom of the pan, which adds bitterness and changes the colour of the khoya. I found out by accident that the burnt milk flavour adds a certain smokiness to khoya, which isn't all that bad. Making khoya does take time and there's a bit of a knack to it, so keep practising! There are many cheat versions using dried milk in a microwave or substituting milk with ricotta cheese (which works well). But if you have the time, try the following recipe.

1 litre/1¾ pints/4 cups whole milk
In a heavy-based saucepan, bring the milk to a boil. Keep stirring and scrape any dried milk from the sides of the pan, stirring it into the boiling milk. Keep cooking on a low heat until the milk reaches the consistency of mashed potatoes or ricotta cheese (around 45 minutes). Allow to cool in the pan. Transfer to an airtight container and refrigerate until needed. Use within a week.

Malai / Pakistani clotted cream

Growing up, the only milk we had was fresh buffalo's milk delivered daily from a local farmer in large stainless steel urns. My mother would find many uses for the milk and its by-products. She would boil the milk to sterilise it, then leave it to cool. While the milk cooled, a rich, thick skin formed on its surface and slowly full cream would rise to join this skin and the result would be a thick cream that hardened on the surface of the milk like a frozen lake. As kids, we would love to smear this precious milkiness on toast with honey or rub some on a paratha with sugar. To me, the closest in flavour and consistency in the West is clotted cream. You can't get Pakistani malai abroad, but what you can do is either substitute it with clotted cream, or make a thickened cream at home. You can then use it as a topping, garnish or a side – some Pakistani desserts would be naked without it. It's an indulgence for special days, especially if you flavour it with rose water, orange blossom water, kewra or honey.

250ml/9 fl oz/generous I cup double (heavy) cream
50ml/2 fl oz/scant ¼ cup sour cream
Combine the ingredients in a small heavy-based saucepan. Slowly bring to the boil, stirring continuously. Lower the heat right down and simmer for 5 minutes. Pour into a heat-resistant bowl and allow to cool. Once cool, cover and wrap it up in a tea towel overnight. In the morning it should be thick and resemble clotted cream. Refrigerate and use within 2 days.

Burutz / lassi cheese
This cheese is made in the mountainous Hunza in two ways. One way involves making a thick lassi from yogurt and milk and filtering this through a cheesecloth until only the solids remain. A quicker way is to heat the lassi over a low heat until the milk splits and solids form around the whey. It is then hung in a cheesecloth until all the whey drips away. I usually just substitute this with a curd-based cheese. It's lovely served with dried fruit and fresh seasonal fruit, as is the norm in the north. See p111 for the method.

Chhana / soured milk cottage cheese
This is probably the most popular cheese for use in desserts, and is just as delicious when eaten on its own. Here's how I make mine.

I litre/1¾ pints/2 cups whole milk
In a heavy-based saucepan, bring the milk to a boil. Once boiling, turn the heat to low and add 2–3 tablespoons of lemon juice and stir. When the whey and milk solids separate, turn the heat off and keep stirring. When all the solids appear to have separated, pour the mixture through a cheesecloth and elevate this over a colander (I tend to tie the cheesecloth onto the kitchen tap with the colander in the sink below). Let the whey drip overnight. In the morning, you'll find a firm cottage cheese. Consume within I day.

Buttery

Ghee / clarified butter
Most of our desserts are cooked in ghee (clarified butter). This can be bought ready made, but making your own doesn't take much time and the flavour is far more authentic. My mother used to make it by collecting the top cream off boiled whole milk and then cooking it down until the milk solids separated and the oil rose. This is pure desi ghee, translating as 'clarified butter of the land'. I make an easier version using unsalted butter, as below.

250g/9oz/I cup unsalted butter
Heat the butter in a saucepan over a low heat until it has entirely melted and scum rises to the top (this can take anywhere between 25 and 40 minutes). Skim occasionally, until all scum stops rising. Allow to cool slightly before pouring through a sieve into a sterilised, heatproof storage jar with a lid. Allow to cool completely before closing the lid. Keep at room temperature and use within 10–15 days. Alternatively, keep for up to 3 weeks in the fridge.

Vegetable oil
Some desserts call for oil, either for frying or cooking with. Try to use one with a subtle aroma, like sunflower or corn.

Makhan and kuch / homemade butter from cream or lassi
Makhan is another milk-based product made from buffalo milk. We would whip the cream that formed on the top of the milk until it thickened and became butter. This was incredible on toast with honey or rose petal jam or on parathas. My friend Moneeza, who is a Pathan, told me about a lassi-based butter called kuch made in her father's village in the north. Salty lassi was made every day in the summer in a huge earthenware pot filled with yogurt, ice and water. This lassi was then hand churned until butter floated to the top. The butter, called kuch, was eaten with simple vegetables and roti or spread over parathas. It can be made in a small blender at home.

350ml/12 fl oz/1½ cups whole plain yogurt
To the full fat yogurt, add 2 trays of ice cubes, 150ml/5 fl oz/ ⅔ cup freezing cold water and a pinch of salt. Blend until you have a lassi. Leave to stand and very soon you will see butter rising to the surface. Pour the whole mixture through a cheesecloth over a colander and squeeze out all the liquid until all you have left is the butter. This takes a little patience, but the flavour is worth it.

Sour morning berries
Rising to mouth-watering spice

Sultry summer mornings would always bring the distant cries of the falsa-wala resonating over the rickshaws, the early song of the cockerel and the warm salty breeze through the half-opened window easing me out of sleep.

On days like this, sweet-sour falsa berries can awaken the senses in a single bite. They are small, purple and unassuming, tossed or juiced in a piquant spice blend, and have a flavour resembling a cross between raspberries and pomegranates. They are the true essence of a summer breakfast in my parents' Karachi home. With the promise of this fresh juice (alongside mango jam, sweet semolina halva and puri breads), I would rise in anticipation of these enticing flavours.

Breakfasts in Pakistan are a mix of enriched local breads, spiced and herbed eggs and fresh fruit – the fruit provides a decadent celebration of the seasons. In summer, watermelons, mulberries, figs, cherries and mangoes are on offer giving way to autumnal pomegranates, apples, apricots and plums. No breakfast table is without some representation of seasonality. Cereals are made from wheat and barley, breakfast sweets include roasted vermicelli in milk and sugar, buckwheat pancakes from the rugged north, and sago pudding eaten during Ramazan. Wherever you eat breakfast in Pakistan, the go-to drink is tea in some form – the southern summer suits a spiced chai, while the extreme northern winter marries well with salted, buttery tea or kehva (green tea).

Breakfast isn't a time for a quick bite on the go, it's a meal taken seriously. It's a time to rise to mouth-watering sweet spices and a meal to treasure with family.

Whipped semolina halva

with pomegranate and raspberry

Semolina halva is a classic Pakistani sweet breakfast, eaten alongside deep-fried puris, savoury chickpeas and spicy potatoes, which sets you up for the whole day. This recipe is a celebration of a classic dish with a Western twist of summer berries. Whisking the halva makes the semolina light and fluffy.

For the raspberry and pomegranate sauce
1 pomegranate, seeds only
150g/generous 1 cup/5½ oz raspberries
2 tbsp caster (superfine) sugar

For the whipped semolina
2 tsp salted butter
2–3 cardamom pods, seeds removed and finely ground
50g/1¾ oz/¼ cup fine semolina
500ml/17 fl oz/2 cups whole milk
150ml/5 fl oz/⅔ cup water (you may not need all of it)

To decorate
extra raspberries and pomegranate seeds
1 tbsp desiccated (dry unsweetened) coconut or coconut shavings
1 tsp toasted buckwheat groats
1 tbsp chopped pistachios

Preparation 15 minutes | **Cooking** 20 minutes | **Serves** 3–4

For the sauce, cook the pomegranate seeds, raspberries and sugar in a small saucepan over a low heat for 5–7 minutes until soft. Once combined and soft, mash the mixture with the back of the spoon, then it push through a sieve to extract all the seeds, adding a little water (about 2 tablespoons) if it is too thick to push through the sieve.

Next, make the semolina. Heat a saucepan over a low heat. When hot, add the butter, and once melted, add the ground cardamom and fry for 5 seconds. Add the semolina and stir until the cardamom and butter has combined with the semolina.

Now, slowly start to add the milk, a little at a time, whisking it into the semolina with a metal whisk until combined, adding a little of the water as the semolina begins to absorb the liquid. Turn the heat to very low. The semolina should begin to thicken and become fluffy. Keep whisking for 2 minutes, then add the raspberry and pomegranate sauce.

Eat warm or chill the semolina for 1 hour in the fridge, if you like. Decorate with the fruit, coconut, buckwheat and pistachios before serving in bowls.

Sharbat

Buckwheat porridge with pink salt, cardamom
and stewed Hunza apricots

*This porridge is based on sharbat, a dish traditionally made with whole grains
and butter for weddings in Hunza and Gilgit in northern Pakistan. I've adapted it
slightly, but it's inspired by the produce grown and eaten in these regions including
the luscious Hunza apricots, which are dried in the sun to preserve them for the
year ahead.*

For the apricots
50g/1¾ oz/⅓ cup dried
   Hunza apricots
1 tbsp caster (superfine)
   sugar or 1 tbsp honey

For the buckwheat porridge
250ml/9 fl oz/generous 1
   cup whole or almond milk
½ tsp pink salt
3 cardamom pods, seeds
   removed
40g/1½ oz/scant ½ cup
   buckwheat flakes

To decorate
1 tbsp chopped pistachios

Preparation 20 minutes + overnight soaking + 1 hour chilling
Cooking 30 minutes | **Serves** 3–4

First, soak the apricots in a bowl of water overnight.

The next day, drain the apricots and remove the stones. Put the sugar or
honey into a saucepan, add the soaked apricots and cook over a very low
heat for 20 minutes. Take off the heat and allow to cool, then chill in the
fridge for at least 1 hour, or overnight.

When you are ready to make the porridge, put the milk, pink salt,
cardamom seeds and buckwheat flakes into another saucepan and place
over a medium heat. Cook, stirring slowly until the porridge thickens.

To serve, pour the buckwheat porridge into bowls, top with the chilled
stewed apricots and sprinkle with chopped pistachios.

Spiced fruit chaat

with guava, pomegranate and mango

Summers would mean walks along the beach, stopping to grab a bite from an array of street food stalls, and fruit chaat was always a favourite. This sweet, spiced fruit salad is a real representation of the flavours of Pakistani street food – fast, seasonal, tangy and fresh.

For the chaat masala

2 tbsp cumin seeds
1–2 dried red chillies
1 tbsp kalamanak (black salt)
1½ tbsp mango powder
   (amchoor)
1 tsp ground anardana (dried
   pomegranate)
1 tsp black peppercorns
   (optional)

For the fruit salad

2–3 large ripe mangoes,
   peeled
4 pink guavas, fresh
   or canned
juice of ½ lime
3 tsp chaat masala or
   more (see above)
½ tsp caster
   (superfine) sugar
2 pomegranates, seeds
   removed
3–4 mint leaves, finely
   chopped

Preparation 15 minutes + 30 minutes chilling | **Serves** 2–3

For the chaat masala, dry-roast the cumin seeds and dried chillies separately in a dry frying pan until fragrant. Transfer to a dry spice grinder, add the remaining ingredients and grind to a powder. Store the excess masala in an airtight jar and keep in a cool, dry place, for up to 1 month.

To make the fruit salad, chop the mangoes and guavas into bite-sized pieces. Juice the lime over the fruit, toss then add the chaat masala and sugar and toss again. Cover and chill in the fridge for about 30 minutes. Decorate with the pomegranate seeds and mint and serve.

Sweet vermicelli pudding

with black cardamom and vanilla

Though roasted vermicelli puddings are usually a part of Eid celebrations, I find this porridge-style version perfect for breakfast. The smoky black cardamom and vanilla are a match made in heaven and remind me of breakfasts in the dry, cool Karachi winter air, sitting out in my grandparents' garden that was filled with seasonal fruits and trees.

50g/1¾ oz roasted vermicelli (seviyan), finely crushed
1 black cardamom pod
¾ tsp vanilla extract
250–300ml/9–10 fl oz/ generous 1–1¼ cups whole milk or unsweetened almond milk
honey, to sweeten (optional)

To decorate
handful of dried cherries or raisins
1 tsp finely ground pistachios

Preparation 10 minutes | **Cooking** 12–15 minutes | **Serves** 2–4

Place the crushed vermicelli, cardamom pod, vanilla and milk in a saucepan and bring to the boil over a medium–low heat. As it comes to the boil, the vermicelli will begin to thicken quickly. If it starts to stick to the pan, add a little more milk and keep stirring until it is thick and the vermicelli is cooked through, about 10 minutes in total.

Serve the vermicelli hot in bowls with a little honey to sweeten, if you like. Scatter the dried cherries or raisins over the top, then dust with finely ground pistachios.

Hunza barove giyaling

Buckwheat pancakes with summer berries, walnuts
and apricot oil

*Salted tea with pancakes – not something people would think of as a Pakistani
breakfast, but in the Hunza valley and Kalash in Chitral you find children huddled
up on floor mats by the soft morning light, enjoying buckwheat pancakes and hot
tea stirred with local pink salt and sometimes a knob of butter. Buckwheat is a
glutinous flour, so there is no need for egg in this recipe. Try making the pancake
as thin as possible to avoid it becoming too heavy.*

300g/10½ oz/2½ cups
   buckwheat flour
400–450ml/14–16 fl oz/1¾–
   2 cups lukewarm water
a pinch of salt
2–3 tbsp apricot kernel oil
   or walnut or almond oil

To serve
2–3 tbsp mulberry syrup
1 tbsp chopped walnuts
8–10 blackberries,
   blackcurrants and cherries

Preparation 15 minutes | **Cooking** 20 minutes | **Makes** 6–10

Whisk the buckwheat flour, lukewarm water and salt together in a bowl
until a thick batter forms.

Grease a flat pancake pan or frying pan with a little of the apricot kernel oil,
then pour in the batter and allow it to spread over the base of the pan to
make a thin pancake. Cook for 1–2 minutes, or until bubbles appear on the
surface, then flip over to cook the other side for 1 minute. Remove, place in
a foil pouch to keep warm and repeat until you have used up all the batter.

Serve the pancakes rubbed with the remaining apricot kernel oil, a drizzle
of mulberry syrup, chopped walnuts and berries.

Shakarpara

Sweet pastry puffs

'Shakar' is the Urdu word for sugar and these tiny crispy diamond-shaped wheat snacks are perfect with a hot cup of doothpati (cardamom and milk tea). Their counterpart are namakpara ('namak' is salt), which are salty and feature cumin. Both remind me of sitting on my Nani's (maternal grandmother) veranda, sipping tea while listening to the song of the summer birds in her garden. These are great for a mid-morning pick-me-up.

For the pastry
200g/7 oz/1½ cups plain
   (all-purpose) flour
a pinch of salt
50g/1¾ oz/3½ tbsp ghee
   or unsalted butter
about 50ml/2 fl oz/
   scant ¼ cup water
sunflower oil or ghee,
   for deep-frying

For the sugar syrup
200g/7 oz/generous 1 cup
   caster (superfine) sugar
100ml/3½ fl oz/scant ½ cup
   water

To decorate
1 tbsp freshly ground
   cardamom seeds
1 tbsp desiccated (dry
   unsweetened) coconut

Preparation 30 minutes + 15 minutes resting | **Cooking** 30 minutes
Makes 30–40 | **Serves** 6–10

Begin by making the pastry. Sift the flour and salt together into a bowl. Add the ghee or butter and knead with your hands, adding enough of the water to make a firm dough. Cover the dough with a damp tea towel and set aside at room temperature for 15 minutes.

Divide the dough into two pieces, then roll each piece out on a lightly floured work surface into a large thin round circle, about 1½mm (1/16 inch) thick. Cut into horizontal strips, then cut across the other way to make small diamond shapes.

Heat the oil or ghee for deep-frying in a wok to 180°C/350°F, or until a cube of bread browns in 30 seconds. When the oil is hot, turn the heat to low and carefully drop batches of the pastry pieces into the hot oil and fry for 2–4 minutes until light brown all over. Remove with a slotted spoon and drain on kitchen paper. Continue until all the pastries have been cooked.

To make the sugar syrup heat the sugar and water together in a saucepan until the sugar has dissolved. Cook to a double thread stage (see p22).

When the syrup is ready, toss the pastries into the syrup and stir thoroughly until they are coated. As the sugar syrup dries around the pastry, the pastry becomes coated and the syrup dries and turns white. Decorate with the cardamom and coconut, and serve. Or store in a dry airtight container for up to 1 month.

Sweet parathas

filled with date, walnut and milk fudge

The nutty aromas of wholemeal bread flour and the filling of fresh dates and nuts remind me of winter mornings in Karachi. Hot chai and sweet parathas are a classic winter treat and waking up to the smell of these flatbreads is very comforting.

For the filling

1 tbsp white poppy seeds
1 tbsp desiccated (dry unsweetened) coconut
3 cardamom pods, seeds removed and finely crushed
2 tbsp ground walnuts
150g/5½ oz/1 cup soft dark black dates, chopped and puréed
2 tbsp khoya / milk fudge (see p23)
1 tbsp grated jaggery

For the paratha dough

150g/5½ oz/1 cup wholemeal (whole wheat) flour, plus extra for dusting
a pinch of salt
4–5 tbsp ghee, plus extra for greasing
water, as needed

To decorate

icing (confectioners') sugar, for dusting

Preparation 25 minutes + 10 minutes resting | **Cooking** 15 minutes | **Makes** 6–8

First make the filling by dry-roasting the poppy seeds, coconut, crushed cardamom seeds and ground walnuts in a frying pan for 45 seconds–1 minute, tossing them around constantly until fragrant. Allow to cool, then add them to the puréed dates, khoya and jaggery and mix with your hands until it is a thick dough-like consistency. Roll the mixture into 6–8 balls about the size of a heaped tablespoon. Set aside.

Next, make the paratha dough by sifting the flour into a bowl, then add the salt and ghee and slowly add enough water to make a soft dough. Place the dough on a lightly floured work surface and knead until smooth. Once ready, cover with clingfilm and rest at room temperature for 10 minutes.

Form the dough into 6–8 small balls, then shape into 1mm/$\frac{1}{16}$ inch discs either with your hands or on a floured surface with a rolling pin. Place one date ball to the middle of the disc, then close the corners of the dough disc to cover the ball. Roll the discs into parathas on a floured surface with a rolling pin. Repeat until all the discs and filling are used up.

Heat a flat pan, grease it with ghee, then place the paratha on the pan and cook for 3–4 minutes on each side until light brown. Remove from the pan and keep warm under a tea towel or in foil. Repeat until all the parathas are cooked. Serve warm.

Bramble gulgulay

Blackberry doughnuts

As the Sindhi weather turned from summer's dusty monsoons to autumn's crisper freshness, it brought with it my Dadi's (paternal grandmother) gulgulay – she loved slowly frying these spiced doughnuts that celebrate the change of the season. Gulgulay are traditionally flavoured with banana, cardamom and aniseed, and sweetened with jaggery. But I have flavoured these doughnuts with sweet blackberries.

50g/1¾ oz/6 tbsp plain (all-purpose) flour
1 tsp bicarbonate of soda (baking soda)
¼ tsp freshly ground green aniseed
¼ tsp freshly ground cardamom seeds
10–20g/¼–¾ oz/2½ tsp– 1 tbsp plus 2 tsp demerara (raw brown) sugar
7–8 big fat blackberries, crushed with a fork into a rough pulp
2 tbsp crushed pistachios
1–2 tbsp whole milk (if required)
250–300ml/9–10 fl oz/ generous 1–1¼ cups vegetable oil, for shallow-frying, or 400–500ml/ 14–17 fl oz/1¾–2 cups oil, for deep-frying

To decorate
icing (confectioners') sugar, for dusting (optional)
1 tsp finely crushed pistachios
1 tsp freshly ground green aniseed

Preparation 20 minutes + 10 minutes resting | **Cooking** 10 minutes | **Makes** 10–15

Sift the flour into a large bowl, add the bicarbonate of soda and the spices and mix together.

Add the sugar to the crushed blackberries, then pour over the flour mixture. Stir until it comes together into a thick batter. Add the pistachios and if you feel it is too thick (doesn't look like a regular doughnut batter) add a tiny bit of milk. Cover the batter and allow to rest at room temperature for about 10 minutes, or until the batter starts to bubble.

Heat the oil for shallow-frying in a deep frying pan and when hot, turn the heat to very low. Using 2 teaspoons to help shape a ball, drop small spoonfuls of the batter into the hot oil. You can fry in batches of 3–4 spoonfuls at a time. Fry each side for about 1–2 minutes. The doughnuts should puff up slightly and be golden brown and crispy. Remove from the pan and drain on kitchen paper.

These can also be deep-fried. Heat the oil for deep-frying in a wok to 180°C/350°F, or until a cube of bread browns in 30 seconds. Drop the doughnut mixture in spoonfuls in batches as above. When the mixture rises to the surface, fry each side for 1–2 minutes until light brown and crispy. Remove and drain on kitchen paper.

Dust with icing sugar (if using) and finely crushed pistachios and aniseed, and serve hot.

Bakar khani

Sweet puff pastry biscuits

This enriched biscuit is popular in Pakistan during Ramazan – I remember enjoying bakar khani for breakfast with hot milk that had poppy and sesame seeds floating on the surface. The traditional method for making bakar khani is long and labourious as it involves making puff pastry with semolina and flour, which needs time to rise. This is a cheat's version using shop-bought puff pastry, but its authenticity lies in its flavours.

1 tbsp ghee for greasing tray and fingers
320g/11¼-oz packet ready-rolled puff pastry
plain (all-purpose) flour, for dusting
2 cardamom pods, seeds removed and finely ground
1 egg yolk
1 tbsp milk
1 tbsp white poppy seeds
1 tbsp sesame seeds
2 tbsp caster (superfine) sugar

Preparation 20 minutes | **Cooking** 20 minutes | **Makes** 8–10

Preheat the oven to 180°C/350°F/gas mark 4 and grease a baking tray.

Spread out the puff pastry sheet on a lightly floured work surface and cut the pastry lengthways into 2.5cm/1-inch strips.

Sprinkle the ground cardamom over each pastry strip, then rub a tiny bit of ghee on your fingers and roll up the strips until you have a small cylinder. Using your palms, press each cylinder down flat, spreading the corners so that the pastry is a little thinner at the edges compared to the middle of the disc to allow the biscuit to rise in a dome.

Stir the egg yolk and milk together in a small bowl and brush the egg wash over the pastries. Sprinkle with the poppy seeds, sesame seeds and sugar and place on the prepared baking tray.

Bake in the oven for 15–20 minutes until golden brown and puffy. Serve warm or cold. Store in an airtight container for 3–4 days.

Rose and lychee sagodanna pudding

Sago doesn't always conjure up good memories for people in the West – to most it is that tasteless gloppy school dinner dessert, but to me it is sweet spiced pearls of milky comfort. Sagodanna ('danna' translates to 'dots' in Urdu) was my most favourite 'shehri' breakfast, the daybreak meal in the month of Ramazan. My mother always made it with cardamom and coconut, but this version combines lychee and rose to make it into an elegant breakfast.

150g/5½ oz/1 cup tapioca pearls
350ml/12 fl oz/1½ cups milk
150ml/5 fl oz/⅔ cup coconut milk
50ml/2 fl oz/scant ¼ cup water
2 tbsp dried milk powder
2 cardamom pods, seeds removed
200g/7 oz/generous 1 cup caster (superfine) sugar
180g/6-oz can lychees, in heavy syrup
50ml/2 fl oz/scant ¼ cup rose syrup

To decorate
8 dried rose petals
1 tbsp slivered pistachios
canned lychees

Preparation 10 minutes + overnight soaking + 5 hours chilling
Cooking 20 minutes | **Serves** 4

Wash the tapioca pearls, then soak in a bowl of water for 1 hour, or overnight.

The next day, drain the tapioca, discard the soaking water and place the tapioca in a saucepan with the milks, water, milk powder, cardamom seeds, sugar and lychee syrup (set the lychees aside). Cook over a medium heat for 15 minutes until the tapioca is cooked through and transparent. Add half the lychees and the rose syrup, then turn the heat to low and cook for another 5 minutes.

Pour the tapioca into a serving dish and allow to cool completely before chilling in the fridge for 4–5 hours before serving. When ready to serve, decorate with rose petals, slivered pistachio and lychees.

Sugar almonds and buffalo milk

The sweetness of diversity

A family weekend trip to Karachi's Hyderabad Colony was an intoxicating experience. The air would be spiced with red onion samosa and biryani, sweet shops brimmed with saffron bread pudding and delicately made rose water marzipan. I looked forward to this trip almost more than any other, as the cuisine is so different from the one cooked at my home, yet it was such a part of my culinary landscape.

I didn't notice any multi-ethnic culinary influences in my cooking until I moved away from home. As I slowly started to crave Hyderabadi sweets, Parsi custards and Kashmiri puddings, I realised that this was because the flavours of the diverse communities that make up Karachi were deeply imbedded in my memories of enjoying meals with friends. Their food culture was as much a part of my childhood as it was theirs.

My circle of friends was as diverse as my home city and the food we shared would reflect our backgrounds. Parsi nankhatai (spiced semolina shortbread), and Hyderabadi khubani ka meetha (stewed apricots with cream and custard) were shared while Bohri friends would surprisingly begin the meal with a dessert of malida (wheat and jaggery dessert). For my part, my father's family were muhajirs (Muslim Indian migrants) that make up a huge part of Karachi's diversity, and my desserts to this day are heavily influenced by the Mughal style of sweetmeats and decadent halvas.

The celebration of food in Pakistan unifies the many cultures that exist in the country, and this is most evident in our dessert culture. Many of the recipes in this chapter have been inspired by the flavours I grew up with in Karachi.

Badam ki jali

Cardamom and rose water marzipan lace

This Hyderabadi sweetmeat translates as 'almond lace' and the name conjures up visions of delicate white fairytale lace. It's a festive sweet for celebrations and gifts. The art is in its making as the traditional methods are laborious and badam ki jali is always made in abundance. The mixture resembles marzipan, but it dries out quickly so you must work fast.

1kg/2¼ lb/7¾ cups almonds with skin on
2 tsp rose water
1kg/2¼ lb/5½ cups caster (superfine) sugar
4–6 cardamom pods, seeds removed and ground
butter, for greasing
500g/1 lb 2 oz/3½ cups icing (confectioners') sugar, for rolling

To decorate
edible silver or gold leaf
15g/½ oz/⅛ cup ground pistachios

Preparation 30–40 minutes + overnight soaking | **Cooking** 10–15 minutes
Makes 8–10

Soak the almonds in a bowl of water overnight. The next day, the skins should come off effortlessly.

Place the almonds in a food processor with the rose water and grind until they are very fine and paste-like, then place in a heavy-based saucepan and add the caster sugar and ground cardamom. Cook over a very low heat, stirring occasionally, until the mixture thickens and leaves the sides of the pan. Transfer the mixture to a greased glass dish, cover with clingfilm and allow to cool to the touch.

Now form the mixture into 2 balls. Roll each ball out as thinly as possible, dusting both the board and the rolling pin liberally with icing sugar. Using a 5–7.5cm/2–3-inch cookie cutter (flower shape is best) cut out 16–20 shapes. Divide the shapes into two equal groups. On one of the groups, cover the surface of the biscuits with silver or gold leaf. Then using a tiny cookie cutter (such as hearts), make holes in the middle of each shape in the second group. Place these on top of the silver or gold leaf covered ones.

Dust with ground pistachios and serve or store in an airtight container for 2–4 days.

Gajrela

Carrot rice pudding

This is a festive pudding that to me unifies the flavours of Karachi. The origins of this dessert are from the Punjab, but there are many different recipes for it in different communities. My favourite by far is this delicious carrot and rice version, which is made in the winter when carrots in Pakistan are deep red, crunchy and intensely sweet. It is one my Nani (maternal grandmother) always made.

100g/3½ oz/½ cup basmati rice
1 litre/1¾ pints/4 cups whole milk
4 cardamom pods, seeds removed and crushed
6 carrots, peeled and grated
2 tbsp ghee or unsalted butter
250g/9 oz/scant 1½ cups caster (superfine) sugar
150ml/5 fl oz/⅔ cup thick double (heavy) cream, to serve

To decorate
2 tbsp chopped almonds, cashews or pistachios
2–3 tbsp desiccated (dry unsweetened) coconut
1 tbsp raisins

Preparation 35 minutes + overnight soaking | **Cooking** 1 hour | **Serves** 6–8

Soak the rice in a bowl of water overnight. The next day, drain the rice and set aside.

Bring the milk to the boil in a heavy-based saucepan, then turn the heat down to medium–low and simmer for about 20 minutes, or until the milk begins to thicken (around 25 minutes), stirring every 1–2 minutes with a wooden spoon to stop the milk sticking to the base of the pan. Add the crushed cardamom seeds and keep stirring. Do not allow the milk to boil. Add the rice and simmer over a low heat for about 15–20 minutes, until the rice is soft and cooked.

Meanwhile, dry-roast the grated carrots in a separate pan over a low heat for 2–3 minutes, or until they begin to wilt, then add the ghee or butter and stir-fry vigorously. When the carrots turn dark (about 3–5 minutes), add the sugar and stir until it is combined (about 2–3 minutes).

Add the carrots to the rice and milk mixture and keep stirring. Turn the heat to its lowest setting and, using a hand-held stick blender, blend the mixture briefly until the carrots and rice are slightly broken down. Increase the heat to high and cook, stirring vigorously for 2–3 minutes.

You can serve this hot or cold. If serving hot, pour into bowls and decorate. If serving cold, allow it to cool in a serving dish and then decorate. Either way, serve with thick cream on the side.

Kishmish paneer

Fresh curd cheese with raisins and sultanas

My mother had an Afghani friend who would always come to our house for a cup of afternoon tea. I never met her family, and the only thing I remember is that she always brought her homemade chewy cheese. Its texture was nothing like any other local cheese — it was firm and reminded me of a sponge, without any saltiness or sweetness, just a pure milkiness. I was told it was an Afghani teatime tradition to serve this with dark black raisins and seasonal fruit.

1 litre/1¾ pints/4 cups whole milk
4 tbsp white wine vinegar or lemon juice
½ tsp salt
250g/9 oz/1¾ cups black or brown raisins
100g/3½ oz/¾ cup sultanas (golden raisins)
any fresh fruit, if desired

Preparation 15 minutes + 20 minutes draining + 2 hours chilling
Cooking 20–25 minutes | **Serves** 4–6

Pour the milk into a non-stick heavy-based pan and, using a whisk, keep stirring the milk while bringing it to the boil. Slowly, add the vinegar or lemon juice and whisk in a circular motion to allow the curds to separate from the whey.

Add the salt and turn off the heat. Whisk in a circular motion for about 5 minutes, or until the curds separate as much as possible from the whey. Line a colander with a muslin cloth and place the colander over the sink. Pour the whey and curds into the muslin, then gather up the corners of the cloth and hold them above the tap. Run cold water through the cloth to wash the vinegar flavour off. Then form the curd into a ball within the cloth. Squeeze the excess liquid through the cloth until the cheese is soft.

Tie the cloth so that it hangs on the tap and allow to drain over the sink completely for about 20 minutes or so. Then leaving the cheese in the cloth, refrigerate for 2 hours until solid.

Serve slices of the cheese with raisins and fresh fruit, if you like. Store the cheese in the fridge for about 2–3 days.

Kashmiri phirin

Ground rice pudding with saffron

Kashmiri food is ceremonial, plentiful and full of flavour. I was used to eating a thick rice pudding called kheer or ground rice firni, but this is a slower-cooked Kashmiri version where whole grains of rice are soaked overnight and then ground. It is traditionally served in unglazed terracotta dishes and usually as a dessert at the end of a wedding meal.

100g/3½ oz/½ cup basmati rice
a pinch of saffron threads
1 tbsp hot milk
500ml/17 fl oz/2 cups whole milk
3–4 cardamom pods, seeds removed and ground
a pinch of salt
50g/1¾ oz/5¾ tbsp icing (confectioners') sugar

To decorate
1 tsp finely ground pistachios
1 tbsp blanched almonds, dry-roasted and roughly chopped
1 tbsp pomegranate seeds
edible silver or gold leaf (optional)

Preparation 20 minutes + overnight soaking + 2–3 hours chilling
Cooking 20 minutes | **Serves** 4–6

Soak the rice in a bowl of water overnight. The next day, soak the saffron in the hot milk for about 15 minutes. Meanwhile, drain the soaked rice and and grind it finely in a food processor. Don't add any water.

Pour the milk into a heavy-based pan and bring to the boil. Add the ground rice, saffron and ground cardamom and cook, stirring constantly until the milk thickens. Add the salt and icing sugar, then turn off the heat and stir.

Pour the rice pudding into serving bowls and chill in the fridge for 2–3 hours. When ready to serve, decorate with ground pistachios, chopped almonds, pomegranate seeds, silver or gold leaf and rose petals, if you like.

Bejewelled Parsi wedding custard

Custards are not really a typical Pakistani dessert, but this Zoroastrian/Parsi celebratory one is called 'lagan nu custard' and is flavoured with nutmeg and cardamom and topped with dried fruit, nuts and rose petals. It's eaten mostly at wedding parties, but sometimes at the end of a Sunday meal.

1½ litres/2½ pints/6⅓ cups whole milk
200ml/7fl oz/scant 1 cup condensed milk
200g/7 oz/generous 1 cup caster (superfine) sugar
ghee or butter, for greasing
4 small eggs
1 tsp vanilla extract
¼ tsp ground nutmeg
3–4 cardamom pods, seeds removed and ground

To decorate
a handful each of whole cashews, blanched almonds, finely chopped pistachios, raisins, dried apricots and dried rose petals

Preparation 15 minutes + 2–4 hours chilling
Cooking 1 hour 15 minutes | **Serves** 8–10

Bring the milk to the boil in a non-stick heavy-based saucepan. As soon as it is boiling turn the heat down to low and add the condensed milk and sugar. Stir for 15 minutes until the sugar has dissolved and the milk is thick and sticky. Remove from the heat and allow to cool.

Preheat the oven to 110°C/220°F/gas mark ¼ and grease a 20 × 15cm/8 × 6-inch baking dish. Using a balloon whisk, beat the eggs, vanilla, nutmeg and ground cardamom in a steel bowl until frothy.

The milk should be tepid before you attempt to stir in the eggs. Slowly stir the eggs in and once it is all combined, pour into the prepared baking dish and bake in the oven for about 1 hour, or until the custard is set and the top is brown.

Allow to cool a little, then chill in the fridge for about 2–4 hours. Decorate with nuts, raisins, and rose petals to serve.

Rabri kulfi sticks

with honey, cardamom and bay leaf

As a child, I remember when the school bell rang we would all run out to follow the kulfi-walla's dilapidated wooden cart. On it, there were beaten steel tubs filled with silver moulds which were tapped to reveal the cold milky pops wrapped in white parchment paper and shrouded in cold mist. Breathing in the sweet smell of kulfi (a fresh full-cream cheese-based ice cream), you could taste it before you peeled off the wrapping. These kulfi ice creams are usually made with fresh rabri (milk solids), but you can use shop bought ricotta instead.

400g/14-oz can condensed milk
1 litre/1¾ pints/4 cups whole milk
4 tbsp ricotta cheese
5 tbsp dried whole milk powder
1 tbsp cornflour (cornstarch)
5–6 cardamom pods, seeds removed
1 bay leaf
1 tbsp honey

To decorate
2 tbsp ground pistachios
1 tbsp white and black poppy seeds

Preparation 15 minutes + overnight freezing | **Cooking** 5–6 minutes
Serves 6–8

Blend the condensed milk, milk, cheese, milk powder, cornflour and cardamom seeds together in a food processor until combined, then pour the mixture into a saucepan and heat over a low heat. Add the bay leaf and honey and heat through until warm. Once the mixture is warm take off the heat. If necessary, adjust the sweetness by adding more honey. Allow the mixture to cool to room temperature.

Pour the cooled mixture into kulfi moulds, seal and place in the freezer overnight. I also use cones made from greaseproof paper, stand them upright in a glass and pour the mixture to the top. I semi-freeze these before sticking in the lolly sticks.

When ready to serve, if using moulds, place them under warm water to ease the kulfi out of the mould. If using the greaseproof paper moulds, just peel the paper gently away to reveal your kulfi on a stick, then dip them into the ground pistachios and poppy seeds to decorate.

Dar ni puri
Sweet bread filled with channa daal and candied peel

I used to have a wonderful Parsi piano teacher who was as passionate about playing Rachmaninoff as she was about her afternoon cup of chai. Many times on weekend lessons I would walk into her house craving these sweet split chickpeas, candied peel and mace-flavoured thick round breads which she would dip into her tea with her elegant long fingers. They're traditionally made with toor daal (split pigeon peas), but I like to use chaana daal in my recipe.

For the filling
200g/7 oz/1 cup channa daal
3 tbsp ghee
150–200g/5½–7 oz/1 cup caster (superfine) sugar
2 tbsp chopped almonds
1 tbsp pine nuts
¼ tsp grated nutmeg
½ tsp ground cardamom
¼ tsp mace
1 tsp rose water
2 tbsp candied peel

For the puri pastry
200g/7 oz/1½ cups plain (all-purpose) flour, plus extra for dusting
1 tbsp icing (confectioners') sugar
1 tbsp ghee
water, as needed

For the glue/maan
2 tbsp plain (all-purpose) flour
3 tbsp ghee

ghee, for frying
1 tbsp desiccated (dry unsweetened) coconut, for sprinkling

Preparation 30–40 minutes + overnight soaking + 2 hours resting
Cooking 25 minutes | **Serves** 6–8

To make the filling, soak the channa daal in a bowl of water overnight. The next day, drain the daal and boil in a pan of fresh water for 25 minutes, or until softened. Drain and set aside.

Heat the ghee in a saucepan over a low heat, add the cooked daal with the sugar and mash with the back of a wooden spoon. Once well combined, add the nuts, spices, rose water and peel, stir well, then allow to cool completely. Using damp hands, roll the cooled mixture into 7.5cm/3-inch diameter balls and set aside on a plate covered with clingfilm or a tea towel.

To make the puri pastry, mix all the ingredients together in a bowl, adding enough water to make a soft dough. Cover with a wet cloth and allow to rest at room temperature for 2 hours.

When ready to make the puri, on a floured surface roll the dough out into 6–8 large discs, about 15–18cm/6–7 inches in diameter and 5mm/¼ inch thick. Mix the flour and ghee together in a bowl to use as a glue – if it becomes solid, sprinkle with water to stop it from drying out. Place a ball of the filling in the centre and flatten it with your fingers until it is 5mm/¼ inch thick, leaving at least 5cm/2 inches free at the sides. Bring the sides together and press to close, stick the corners together with glue, then roll out into a 4cm/1½-inch thick disc.

Heat a flat pancake pan or tawa, rub a little ghee on the surface and cook the puri for 7–8 minutes on each side until light brown and the dough is cooked through. Serve hot, sprinkled with coconut.

Roasted nuts and rock sugar

with hazelnuts, dates, dried cherries and chickpea flour

This recipe is inspired by chickpea flour ladoos, which are found at many Hindu weddings in Pakistan. I have used many of the elements of the ladoo to make this granola-style mix, although a nut called charoli is used in many Parsi sweets, and I have added hazelnuts here. The gritty texture of chickpea flour, nuts and cardamom is always so moreish. This is delicious served with yogurt, milk or even on its own.

2 tbsp ghee

2–3 cardamom pods, seeds removed and crushed

4 tbsp grated jaggery or muscovado sugar

50g/1¾ oz/scant ½ cup chickpea (gram) flour

2 tbsp coarse semolina

50g/1¾ oz/¼ cup pitted dates, roughly chopped

1 tbsp chopped pistachios

1 tbsp chopped walnuts

1 tbsp pine nuts

1 tbsp chopped hazelnuts

1 tbsp dried cherries

2 tbsp desiccated (dry unsweetened) coconut

4–5 pieces misri (rock sugar) roughly broken

Preparation 15 minutes | **Cooking** 5 minutes | **Serves** 4

Heat the ghee in a frying pan over a low heat, add the crushed cardamom seeds and as soon as they are aromatic, add the jaggery and allow to melt. Add the chickpea flour and semolina and cook in the melted jaggery, stirring occasionally, for a few seconds, allowing it to form lumps. Add the remaining ingredients and cook for another 30 seconds until fragrant.

Allow to cool, then store in an airtight container for 1 week.

Mango, thyme and pink salt

with rose water clotted cream

This is a delicious combination of the flavours of my childhood: sweet summer mangoes, mineral pink salt, rock hard sugar, gritty poppy seeds and the freshness of garden-picked herbs, topped with decadent fresh whipped buffalo's milk clotted cream or what we call malai – the fresh cream that tops whole boiled unpasteurised milk. Here, I have created a homemade version of malai, which comes pretty close.

For the clotted cream
200ml/7 fl oz/scant 1 cup
  double (heavy) cream
50ml/2 fl oz/scant ¼ cup
  sour cream
1 tbsp honey
2 tsp rose water

For the toppings
2 large ripe mangoes, peeled,
  stoned and sliced
1 tbsp white or black poppy
  seeds
1 tsp pink salt
1 tbsp pistachios, sliced
1 tsp roughly crushed misri
  (rock sugar) or jaggery
a few crushed lemon
  thyme leaves

Preparation 10 minutes + overnight standing | **Cooking** 10 minutes | **Serves** 2–4

Make the clotted cream by bringing the creams and honey to the boil in a heavy-based saucepan very slowly over a very low heat. Turn the heat down and simmer for 5 minutes, then turn off the heat. Allow the cream to cool before adding the rose water.

Pour the mixture into a non-metallic bowl, cover with a couple of thick tea towels and leave overnight at room temperature to thicken. In the morning, refrigerate until ready to use.

Serve with all the toppings on the side.

Memon lappi

Crunchy oats with jaggery, cinnamon and fennel seeds

Traditionally served as a dessert the day after a Memon wedding, this unusual porridge is normally made with cracked wheat, but oats are a wonderful substitute. The fennel flavour marries well with the crunchiness of the oats too.

225g/8 oz/1½ cups jaggery or muscovado sugar, grated or cut into small pieces
400ml/14 fl oz/1¾ cups water
2 tbsp ghee or unsalted butter
2.5cm/1-inch cinnamon stick
3 cardamom pods, seeds removed
50g/1¾ oz/½ cup jumbo oats
3 tsp fennel seeds, roughly crushed
1 tsp slivered pistachios or flaked (slivered) almonds, to decorate

Preparation 10 minutes | **Cooking** 15 minutes | **Serves** 2

Begin by making the jaggery syrup. Heat the jaggery and water in a heavy-based saucepan until the jaggery is completely dissolved, then cook over a low heat for about 4–5 minutes until it is a slightly thick syrup. Turn off the heat and set aside.

Heat the ghee or butter in another saucepan over a medium heat, add the cinnamon stick and cardamom seeds, and when they start to sizzle, add the oats. Stir for about 1–2 minutes until the oats are coated with the ghee and there is a slight nutty smell.

Now add the jaggery syrup, stir and turn the heat down to its lowest setting. Cover the pan and leave to cook in its own steam for 2–4 minutes. Check to see if the jaggery syrup has been absorbed.

Once the jaggery syrup has been absorbed, add the crushed fennel seeds and stir. Cover and leave for 1 minute.

Serve warm with slivered pistachios or almonds and a sprinkle of fennel seeds.

Kites, kingdoms and cardamom samosas

Flavours from Lahore and the Mughal Empire

The Basant Kite Festival in Lahore is one of my favourite Pakistani celebrations. Flashes of mustard yellow and lime green light the sky, smoke billows from a distance carrying with it the aromas of barbecued meat, and the perfume of saffron and cardamom gulab jamun and jalebis fill the senses.

Lahore is a city of enchanting legacy. From the breathtaking Mughal architecture to the streets of the Walled City, it transports you to a bygone era. The area that now hosts Lahore's famous 'food street' used to house the 'dancing girls' of Lahore, but now it is alive with the aromas of freshly made tandoori bread as the scent of agarbatti (incense) mixes intoxicatingly with rose syrup or saffron from falooda, sweetmeats or samosas. This is a city that lies within the agricultural province of Punjab, ensuring that there is never a dearth of seasonal vegetables and fruits.

Lahoris feast like kings. They start the day with a decadent breakfast, at teatime they have mithai (sweetmeats) and dinner with hot jalebis and sweet cardamom samosas, while eating goes on late into the night. This is a city where you can enjoy a cup of hot cardamom chai with firni at midnight overlooking the mesmerising Badshahi Mosque or Lahore Fort, oozing Mughal romanticism.

A city of such beauty and flavour deserves a celebration of its own, so the recipes in this chapter are influenced by its history, tradition and love of sweets. Some family recipes are included which mingle together with those inspired by the region, but each one aims to capture the dessert flavours of Lahore.

Slow-cooked Lahori kheer rice pudding

There is something very special about this rice pudding – it could be the fragrance of Pakistani basmati and kewra (screwpine extract) slowly simmered in thick full-fat milk or the astringency of cardamom, which cuts through the intense sweetness of the pudding. The comforting, thick goodness of Lahori kheer is the result of perseverance, stirring and a low heat.

180g/6 oz/1 cup basmati rice
150ml/5 fl oz/⅔ cup whole milk, preferably unpasteurised
1 star anise
1cm/½-inch cinnamon stick
2 cardamom pods
1 litre/1¾ pints/4 cups water
a pinch of salt
350g/12 oz/2 cups caster (superfine) sugar
1 tsp kewra (screwpine extract) or 2 tsp rose water

To decorate
almonds, chopped
chopped dried figs

Preparation 15 minutes + overnight soaking | **Cooking** 4 hours | **Serves** 6

Soak the rice in a bowl of water overnight. The next day, drain the rice and set aside.

Bring the milk to the boil in a heavy-based cast-iron saucepan. Add the spices, turn the heat down and simmer for 30 minutes until the milk becomes thick. Keep checking that it doesn't burn on the base of the pan.

Bring the water to the boil in another saucepan. Add the salt and the soaked rice and boil for about 7–10 minutes, or until it is cooked. Strain and add the cooked rice to the milk. Turn the heat down to its lowest setting and place on a diffuser, if you have one. If not just keep it on a very low heat. Slow-cook the rice pudding for 3–4 hours, stirring frequently and checking occasionally to make sure that the milk remains at least 5cm/ 2 inches below the rim of the pan and doesn't catch and burn on the pan.

After 3–4 hours, the rice and milk will be thick and gloopy. Add the sugar and stir until it has dissolved, then turn off the heat and stir in the kewra or rose water

Remove and discard the whole spices from the rice pudding, then decorate with nuts and figs and serve warm or cold.

Sohan saffron honey caramels

with rose water, pistachio and almonds

Sipping black coffee with a honeyed sohan caramel is my first grown-up memory of flavour. My mother used to make these from a recipe given to her by a Persian lady who lived in Lahore. The chewy caramel with saffron gracing each bite is made even more distinctive by the crunch of nuts. In Pakistan, we also have multani sohan, a halva made with sprouted wheat, which is said to have links to this Persian one. To me, this version is more pleasurable as the sticky sweetness remains long after that first bite.

a pinch of saffron threads
1 tbsp boiling water
180g/6 oz/1 cup caster (superfine) sugar
60g/2¼ oz/¼ cup unsalted butter, roughly chopped
5 tbsp clear honey
140g/5 oz/1¾ cups flaked (slivered) almonds
2 tsp rose water
vegetable oil, for oiling
60g/2¼ oz/½ cup shelled pistachios, finely chopped
1 tbsp dried rose petals

Preparation 20 minutes + 15 minutes soaking + 1 hour cooling
Cooking 15 minutes | **Makes** 10–15

Line 2 baking trays with greaseproof paper. Soak the saffron in the boiling water for 15 minutes.

Meanwhile, place the sugar, butter and honey in a saucepan over a medium heat, but do not mix, and allow the sugar to dissolve. Once completely dissolved, add the almonds and cook until the mixture reaches a triple thread stage or 140°C/284°F on a sugar thermometer.

Remove the pan from the heat and immediately add the saffron and its soaking water. Be careful as the hot caramel will spit. Taking the handle of the saucepan, swirl the contents around quickly to combine, then add the rose water.

Working really quickly, use an oiled wooden spoon to spoon the mixture onto the greaseproof paper, spacing the blobs well apart, then pat them down to form 10–15 small round discs about 10–13cm/4–5 inches in diameter. Sprinkle on the pistachios and rose petals, then allow the caramels to cool at room temperature for 1 hour or so.

Once cooled and hardened, store in an airtight container for 7–10 days.

Pakistani jalebis
Spiralled fermented doughnuts in turmeric-infused syrup

On every roadside in Pakistan, muslin bags are filled with fermented batter ready to form these bright orange spiralled doughnuts that dance on the surface of black cast-iron cauldrons of hot oil, and are quickly scooped up and thrown into syrup. Their texture is multidimensional – hot, sticky to touch and crisp to bite. I always looked forward to staying with my cousins in Lahore and having either a midnight treat of milky chai with fresh jalebis and late-night chats, or a breakfast of cold jalebis with hot milk. A labour of love, these are definitely worth the effort.

a pinch of saffron threads
1 tbsp hot water or milk
125g/4½ oz/1 cup minus
   1 tbsp plain (all-purpose)
   flour
2 tbsp rice or chickpea flour
½ tsp bicarbonate of soda
   (baking soda)
175ml/6 fl oz/¾ cup whole
   plain yogurt, or 120ml/
   4 fl oz/½ cup buttermilk
2 tbsp ghee, melted
¼ tsp ground turmeric
water, as needed
vegetable oil, for deep-frying
1 tbsp desiccated (dry
   unsweetened) coconut,
   for sprinkling

For the sugar syrup
240ml/8 fl oz/1 cup water
200g/7 oz/generous 1 cup
   caster (superfine) sugar
¼ tsp ground turmeric
2 tsp lemon juice

NB: This batter gets its airiness from natural fermentation. The traditional leavening agent is plain yogurt, but you can use buttermilk or Greek yogurt.

Preparation 30 minutes + 15 minutes soaking + overnight fermentation
Cooking 30 minutes | **Makes** 10–12

Soak the saffron in the hot water or milk for 15 minutes. Whisk the flours and bicarbonate of soda together in a large bowl. Add the yogurt or buttermilk and melted ghee and stir well to form a thick batter. Add the saffron and turmeric and enough water to make a thick pancake batter. Add a little more flour if you need to.

Cover the bowl with a tea towel and and leave in a warm place to ferment for up to 12 hours, or overnight. The batter should rise and become fluffy.

Next, make the sugar syrup by boiling the water and sugar together in a pan. Cook the syrup until it reaches the single thread stage (see p22), but do not let it burn. Take off the heat and stir in the turmeric and lemon juice. Set aside.

To cook the jalebis, heat enough oil for deep-frying in a heavy-based pan or wok to 190°C/375°F, or until a cube of bread browns in 30 seconds. Pour the batter into a clean squeezy bottle or into a food-grade plastic bag, and cut a small hole in one corner of it when you are ready to make the jalebis.

Using your dispenser, squeeze the batter into the hot oil in coils or spirals that are about 5cm/2 inches wide. Only make 3–4 jalebis at a time and fry for 6–8 minutes until crisp and golden brown. Remove with a slotted spoon and drain on kitchen paper, then drop the jalebis into the syrup for 5 minutes, making sure they are coated all over. They should be sticky and saturated. Jalebis can be eaten hot or at room temperature sprinkled with coconut.

Lahori falooda

Kulfi float with basil seeds, glass noodles and rose syrup

In search of the perfect Lahori falooda, I visited many ice-cream stalls in the city. I finally found the perfect one with just the right balance of flavour, colour and texture. From the creamy green pistachio kulfi with vibrant red rose syrup, through the squishy basil seeds and slippery glass noodles, to the thick sweet condensed milk, this dessert comes together in your mouth in perfect harmony. I use the Peshawari pistachio ice cream on p133 in this recipe.

3 tbsp basil seeds (thukhmalnga) or chia seeds
20g/¾ oz china glass noodles or falooda noodles
200ml/7 fl oz/scant 1 cup condensed milk
4 scoops of Peshawari pistachio ice cream (see p133)
3–4 tbsp rose syrup
1 tbsp chopped pistachios

Preparation 10 minutes + 15 minutes soaking | **Serves** 4

Begin by soaking the basil seeds in a bowl of cold water for about 5 minutes. They will become glutinous and resemble chia seeds. Drain and set aside.

Next, soak the noodles in a heatproof bowl of warm water for about 10 minutes, or until they are rehydrated. Drain and set aside.

To assemble the falooda, place some noodles in the base of a sundae glass, pour over some condensed milk, add some basil seeds, ice cream and rose syrup and decorate with chopped pistachios.

Serve immediately.

Rice flour pancakes
with black cardamom and poppy seeds

One winter's afternoon a friend in Lahore (who is originally from north Pakistan), greeted me with these thin pancakes with homemade cottage cheese and local honey from their farm. They left an indelible flavour memory, so I have recreated them here perfuming them with smoky black cardamom, which complements the rice flour beautifully.

150g/5½ oz/1⅓ cups rice flour
2 tbsp cornflour (cornstarch)
1 tsp caster (superfine) sugar
a pinch of salt
120ml/4 fl oz/½ cup coconut milk
1 black cardamom pod, seeds removed and ground
120ml/4 fl oz/½ cup water
2 tbsp butter, for cooking

To serve
1 tbsp poppy seeds
2 tbsp curd cheese (see p56)
2 tbsp honey

Preparation 15 minutes | **Cooking** 35 minutes | **Makes** 10–12

Whisk all the ingredients together, except the poppy seeds, cheese, honey and butter, together in a bowl until a thin batter forms.

Heat a little non-stick frying pan, rub a little butter on the surface, then pour a ladleful of the batter into the pan and swirl the batter around the base of the pan to make a thin pancake. Cook on each side for 2–3 minutes until light brown and cooked, and the edges start to curl. Remove from the pan and keep warm in a foil pouch. Repeat until you have used up all the batter.

Serve the pancakes with the cheese, honey and a sprinkling of poppy seeds.

Malpura semolina pancakes

with raspberry and pomegranate sauce

Pakistani malpura pancakes are a festive fried pancake, topped with honey, fruit or syrup. They are shallow-fried in oil until they have crispy edges, but still retain a spongy centre. Here, I have accompanied them with a delicious raspberry and pomegranate sauce (see p31 for the recipe).

150g/5½ oz/scant 1 cup fine semolina
125g/4½ oz/1 cup minus 1 tbsp plain (all-purpose) flour
125g/4½ oz/¾ cup caster (superfine) sugar
3–4 cardamom pods, seeds removed and ground
a pinch of saffron threads
300–425ml/10–15 fl oz/ 1¼– generous 1¾ cups buttermilk
a pinch of bicarbonate of soda (baking soda)
1 tbsp ghee or oil, for frying

To decorate
1 tbsp desiccated (dry unsweetened) coconut
1 tbsp pistachios, chopped
1 tbsp walnuts, chopped
raspberry and pomegranate sauce (see p31)

Preparation 20 minutes + overnight resting | **Cooking** 15 minutes | **Makes** 6–8

Reserve about 2 tablespoons of semolina, then put the remaining semolina, the flour, sugar and spices in a bowl and mix to combine. Add the buttermilk and stir until it forms a batter. Cover with a tea towel and set aside overnight at room temperature.

The next day, stir the reserved semolina and bicarbonate of soda into the batter until combined.

Heat the ghee or oil in a frying pan, add 1 tablespoon of the batter into the pan and swirl to form a 2.5cm/1-inch round pancake. You can make 2–3 pancakes at a time. Shallow-fry the pancakes for 2–3 minutes until the edges are crisp and brown but the centre remains soft. Flip over and cook the other side for another 2–3 minutes. Remove and drain on kitchen paper, then keep in a warm pouch while the rest are cooked.

Serve the pancakes hot, decorated with coconut and nuts, with the sauce on the side (see p31).

Semolina halva ladoos

with buckwheat groats, pine nuts, aniseed and coconut

Ladoos are the quintessential Pakistani mithai (sweetmeat), whether they are made with chickpea flour, moong daal, wheat or my favourite, with semolina. My Nani always made these during Eid. We would also take them with us when visiting family in Lahore and they always managed to stay intact, probably because of the copious amount of ghee that binds them together! These ladoos are a slightly healthier – they are rolled in toasted buckwheat and desiccated coconut.

3–4 tbsp buckwheat groats
50g/1¾ oz/⅔ cup desiccated (dry unsweetened) coconut, plus 2 tbsp dry-roasted desiccated coconut
2 tbsp ghee
165g/5¾ oz/1 cup fine semolina
4 cardamom pods, seeds removed and crushed
½ tsp ground aniseed
2 tbsp chopped pine nuts
400g/14-oz can condensed milk

Preparation 15 minutes + 1 hour setting | **Cooking** 15 minutes | **Makes** 10–12

Dry-roast the buckwheat and the 2 tablespoons of coconut separately in a dry frying pan over a medium heat for 1–2 minutes until light brown. Take the pan off the heat and allow to cool.

Heat the ghee in a frying pan over a medium heat, add the semolina and fry for 5 minutes stirring constantly to prevent it burning. Add the cardamom seeds, ground aniseed, pine nuts, then non-roasted coconut.

Next, add the condensed milk and reduce the heat to low and mix to combine. Cook for 5–8 minutes until the mixture leaves the side of the pan, then take the pan off the heat and allow to cool.

Spread the dry-roasted coconut and the buckwheat groats out on separate plates. Using clean hands, roll the cooled mixture into 10–12 balls, then roll them in the coconut and buckwheat until coated. Allow to set for 1 hour at room temperature.

Serve the balls at room temperature or store in the fridge for up to 3 days.

Mango, cardamom, saffron and red chilli murraba

As a child I would dig a spoon into a whole jar of murraba as a snack after school. Murraba can be made from any fruit, petal or vegetable, and is essentially a sweet concentrate with a hint of exotic saffron, cardamom or pepper. I love this recipe with mangoes and red chilli as it reminds me of taking summer Sindhi mangoes to my family in Lahore, who were rarely able to indulge in the floral intensity of the mangoes from the south.

500g/1 lb 2 oz ripe Pakistani honey mangoes, peeled, stoned and cut into 2.5cm/1-inch strips

50ml/2 fl oz/scant ¼ cup water

300g/10½ oz/1⅓ cups caster (superfine) sugar

3 red chillies, deseeded and cut into strips

4–5 cardamom pods, seeds removed and ground

a large pinch of saffron threads

Preparation 20 minutes | **Cooking** 30 minutes | **Makes** 4–6

First, sterilise 4–6 jam jars. To do this, preheat the oven to 140°C/275°F/gas mark 1. Wash the jars in hot, soapy water, then rinse well. Place them on a baking sheet and put them in the oven to dry completely. If using Kilner jars, boil the rubber seals, as dry heat damages them. Set aside.

Cook the mangoes and water in a pan for 10 minutes, then add the sugar and stir. Cook until the mixture is at the single thread stage (see p22).

Add the chillies, ground cardamom and saffron and continue to cook until the mixture is thick and translucent. It should now beat the double thread stage (see p22). Allow to cool, then pour into the prepared jars. Store for up to 3 months in a cool dry place.

Shakarkandi ki kheer

Sweet potato pudding with rice flour and spices

Thick, creamy and subtle, this kheer made with grated sweet potato and rice flour is total comfort food. Cold Lahori winter trips would include a freshly made bowl of shakarkandi ki kheer made by my aunt. Traditionally it is eaten cold, but I prefer it hot.

500g/1 lb 2 oz sweet potato
1 litre/1¾ pints/4 cups whole milk
6 cardamom pods, bashed to expose seeds
50g/1¾ oz/¼ cup caster (superfine) sugar
2 tbsp rice flour
350ml/12 fl oz/1½ cups condensed milk

To decorate
2 tbsp chopped pistachios
1 tbsp ground pistachios

Preparation 15 minutes | **Cooking** 1 hour | **Serves** 6

Peel the sweet potatoes, then cut them into cubes and boil them in a pan of water for 10–15 minutes until soft. Drain, return to the pan and mash well, then set aside.

Bring the milk and cardamom pods to the boil in a heavy-based saucepan. Turn the heat to very low and cook for 10–15 minutes until the milk starts to become thick. Add the sugar and allow to dissolve, then add the mashed sweet potatoes and stir until the milk and potatoes are well combined.

Mix the rice flour and 2 tablespoons of cold milk together in a small bowl, then add to the sweet potato mixture still on the heat. Keep stirring until it starts to thicken. Add the condensed milk and stir, then cook for 10 minutes until the mixture is thick. Turn off the heat and allow to cool in the pan.

Serve at room temperature, chilled or warm, scattered with the pistachios over the top.

Dahi ki kheer

Baked saffron yogurt

This is a thick baked yogurt best served in a terracotta bowl. I have always loved sweet yogurt, the set kind with body, creaminess and a rich flavour. On a trip to Lahore I enjoyed this baked saffron yogurt at a well-known rooftop Pakistani restaurant overlooking Badshahi Mosque – I fell in love with both the view and the satisfaction of each spoonful of this dessert.

240ml/8 fl oz/1 cup whole milk
500ml/17 fl oz/2 cups evaporated milk
120ml/4 fl oz/½ cup condensed milk
a pinch of saffron threads
1 tbsp ghee
245g/8¾ oz/1 cup whole plain yogurt

Preparation 15 minutes | **Cooking** 1¼–1¾ hours | **Serves** 6–8

Combine the whole milk, evaporated milk and condensed milk together in a bowl and mix well. Add the saffron.

Transfer the mixture to a saucepan and heat over a low heat for 5–7 minutes, or until it is warmed through. Add the ghee and heat until it is melted. Turn off the heat and allow to cool to lukewarm. Whisk in the yogurt and mix well.

Preheat the oven to 200°C/400°F/gas mark 6 for 5 minutes, then lower the temperature to 110°C/220°F/gas mark ¼. Pour the mixture into a terracotta bowl or an ovenproof dish and bake in the oven for 1–1½ hours until firm to the touch. Chill in the fridge and enjoy cold.

Through mulberry valleys
Summer fruits in harsh winters

The rugged splendour and romantic rusticity of northern Pakistan is captivating, but it is the people, and most of all their simple seasonal food, that has always inspired me. The arduous journey through isolated valleys is made easier by the welcoming aromas of smoky wood burners cooking local breads and the fresh mountain breeze carrying with it the scent of brewing qawa (green tea) and sweet dark oranges.

The mountainous regions of Chitral, Swat, Hunza and Gilgit boast snowy peaks during winter, and in late summer and autumn are breathtaking. A view from a height captures a vision of ingeniously irrigated green cornfields weaving through valley floors, the air fragrant with the jasmine-like scent of Russian olives and blackberries, the trees aflame with apricots and mulberries, the mountainsides dotted with large baskets of fruit left to be sun-dried before the harsh barren winter ahead.

The hospitality of the locals is endearing – visitors are greeted with warm honey milk, a dastarkhwan (dining floor mat) laden with walnuts from the trees, plums, figs, ripe cherries or apricots in platters, local cheeses and bread, all washed down with buttery salted tea, while sucking on misri (rock sugar).

Northern Pakistan is hugely diverse: there is deep history to its rustic cuisine, which bears influences of the Silk Road and invaders from other lands. I have always had a personal passion for the region's history and its untouched beauty. Its ethos of eating locally and preserving food for the rest of the year (as well as sharing with friends and family) draws me back to this part of my homeland both in mind and spirit.

Spiced apple samosas

These sweet samosas are inspired by the bountiful supply of apples in the north. They are gently spiced with cinnamon, cardamom and mace, which offer a warm comfort with each mouthful. Apples are also made into murraba (p89) and then eaten through the year.

For the pastry
150g/5½ oz/1 cup plus 2 tbsp plain (all-purpose) flour, plus extra for dusting
a pinch of salt
1 tbsp fine semolina
water, as needed
vegetable oil, for oiling and deep-frying

For the filling
6 Royal Gala apples, peeled, cored and cut into bite-sized pieces
100g/3½ oz/½ cup golden caster (superfine) sugar
¼ tsp ground cinnamon
3–4 cardamom pods, seeds removed and ground
a pinch of ground mace

To serve
150ml/5 fl oz/⅔ cup cream, whipped with 1 tsp rose water
1 tsp dried rose petals

Preparation 25 minutes | **Cooking** 20 minutes | **Makes** 6–8

Begin by making the pastry. Combine the flour, salt and semolina in a bowl, then slowly add enough water to bring all the ingredients together into a dough. Knead the dough on a clean floured work surface and form into a soft dough. Lightly grease your hands with oil, pat the dough down, cover with a damp cloth and allow to rest at room temperature.

Meanwhile, make the filling. Heat a saucepan, add the apples, sugar and spices and cook over a medium-low heat for about 10 minutes, or until the apples are soft, glistening and the sugar is dissolved and shiny. Take off the heat and allow to cool.

Knead the dough on a floured surface, then roll it out to 5mm/¼ inch thick. Using a 5-cm/2-inch diameter round pastry cutter, cut out 6–8 circles.

To fill the samosas, place about 1 teaspoon of the filling for each samosa, on one half of the circle, then fold the dough into half moons and press the corners with a fork to close. When all the samosas are made heat the oil for deep-frying in a large deep frying pan to 180°C/350°F, or until a cube of bread browns in 30 seconds.

Drop the samosas into the hot oil in batches. Deep-fry each samosa for 2–3 minutes on each side, then remove with a slotted spoon and drain on kitchen paper. Serve immediately with whipped cream decorated with rose petals.

Chitrali rishiki

Pancakes with mulberry syrup

These are wheat-based pancakes topped with pine nuts, walnuts and mulberry syrup. On a trip to Chitral I was served these with a homemade sheerni – a laborious slow-cooked black mulberry syrup which takes a whole night to prepare. The end result is an intense and heady flavour. It's treated like liquid gold. If you can't find fresh mulberries or mulberry syrup in the shops, then honey and salty cottage cheese make a great substitute.

250g/9 oz/1¾ cups
   wholemeal (wholewheat)
   flour
a pinch of salt
1 tbsp caster (superfine)
   sugar
2 eggs, well beaten
250ml/9 fl oz/generous
   1 cup whole milk
ghee, for cooking

For the topping
1 tbsp mulberry syrup
1 tbsp walnuts, roughly
   chopped
1 tbsp pine nuts
fresh mulberries
   (or dry mulberries
   or blackberries)

Preparation 15 minutes + 30 minutes resting | **Cooking** 15 minutes | **Makes** 6–8

Sift the flour, salt and sugar together into a large bowl. Make a well in the middle and pour in the beaten eggs, then slowly add the milk and whisk until everything is combined. Cover with a tea towel and set aside for 30 minutes at room temperature.

To make the pancakes, heat a flat pancake pan or a non-stick frying pan over a medium heat. Rub the pan with a little ghee, then pour in a ladleful of the batter. Using the back of the ladle, spread the batter out in circular motions to form a really thin pancake. You will need to do this very quickly as the batter starts to cook immediately.

When you see tiny bubbles on the surface (1 minute) turn over and cook for another 1 minute on the other side. Remove the pancake from the pan and keep warm in a foil pouch. Repeat until all the batter is used up.

Serve the pancakes warm with fresh mulberries, mulberry syrup and nuts.

Chamborogh

Stewed Hunza apricots with cream and apricot kernels

Stewed fruits are very popular in Hunza and Chitral. This recipe is a classic Chitrali dish where fresh or dried apricots are stewed and served with toasted apricot kernels and fresh cream. The simplicity of this dessert is a true representation of the region.

200g/7 oz/1⅓ cups dried Hunza apricots
80g/3 oz/scant ½ cup caster (superfine) sugar
250ml/9 fl oz/generous 1 cup double (heavy) cream, to serve

To decorate
1 tbsp dried cherries
2 tbsp apricot kernels or chopped dry-roasted almonds or walnuts
1 tbsp dried rose petals

Preparation 20 minutes + overnight soaking | **Cooking** 20 minutes
Serves 6–8

Place the apricots in a bowl and pour in enough water to cover. Make sure they are completely submerged. Allow to soak overnight.

The next day, squeeze the stones out of the apricots, then pour the water used for soaking the apricots together with the stoned apricots into a saucepan. Add the sugar and cook over a medium heat for 15–20 minutes, or until the sugar is dissolved and the apricots are glistening. Do not stir. Take off the heat and allow to cool in the pan, then chill completely before serving.

Decorate the chilled apricots with dried cherries, apricot kernels or nuts and rose petals and serve with the cream on the side.

Apple halva
with cardamom and pomegranate

Apples are bountiful during the cooler months in the north, so this is another Chitrali-inspired dessert – apples are cooked down slowly with a sugar syrup to create a thick concentrate and then served cool with whipped cream.

5–6 Royal Gala apples, peeled, cored and cut into bite-sized pieces
2 tbsp ghee
3–4 cardamom pods, seeds removed and crushed
200g/7 oz/generous 1 cup caster (superfine) sugar
150ml/5 fl oz/⅔ cup double (heavy) cream, whipped, to serve

To decorate
a handful of pomegranate seeds
a handful of blanched slivered (flaked) almonds

Preparation 20 minutes + 1 hour chilling | **Cooking** 25–30 minutes | **Serves** 4

Blitz the apple pieces in a food processor until a smooth purée has formed.

Heat the ghee in a saucepan over a medium heat, add the cardamom and apple purée and cook for 15–20 minutes until brown and all the water from the apples has been absorbed.

Next, add the sugar and begin to stir vigorously as the apple starts to thicken and glisten. Keep stirring until the mixture starts to leave the sides of the pan and it is dark brown and shiny.

Transfer the halva to a bowl, cover with clingfilm and allow to cool, then chill in the fridge for at least 1 hour.

When ready to serve, decorate with the pomegranate seeds and almonds and serve cool with whipped cream.

Mulberry and cherry fruit leather

with crushed walnuts and pistachios

Fruit leathers are found in many parts of Pakistan. In the south they are made with mangoes, while in the north they are made from cherries, mulberries or apples. In Chitral and Hunza, you can find these dark, stained glass-like sheets drying in the mountain sun. The locals love to crush walnuts or pistachios finely and spread them on the fruit leathers, then eat them as a snack. This recipe is based on the Chitrali dessert shakarpostik, where dried mulberries and walnuts are ground together and then dried into a fruit leather.

100g/3½ oz/⅔ cup dried black mulberries or Hunza apricots
300g/1½ cup/10½ oz cherries, pitted
50g/1¾ oz/¼ cup caster (superfine) sugar
1 tbsp honey
a pinch of salt
3 tbsp crushed pistachios
3 tbsp crushed walnuts

Preparation 15 minutes + 15 minutes soaking | **Cooking** 2–3 hours | **Serves** 2–3

Soak the mulberries in a heatproof bowl of hot water for 15 minutes, then drain and set aside. If using apricots, soak them overnight, then drain and remove the stones.

Place the cherries, drained mulberries or apricots, sugar and honey in a saucepan and cook over a low heat for about 15 minutes, or until soft and pulpy and the moisture has gone.

Preheat the oven to 90°C/200°F/lowest possible gas mark.

Transfer the mixture to a blender, add the salt and whizz to a purée. Pour 2 tablespoons of the mixture onto a sheet of greaseproof paper and spread it out as thinly as possible with a palette knife. Repeat on separate pieces of greaseproof paper once or twice more. Place each piece of paper on a baking tray and sprinkle the crushed nuts evenly over the mixture. Bake in the oven for 2–3 hours, or until shiny and dry. Remove from the oven and allow to cool completely. Once cool, the fruit leather should peel off easily.

Cut the fruit leather into 5cm/2-inch strips, then roll up and store in an airtight container for 2 weeks.

Mulberry and blackberry stew

This dessert is a celebration of the region. Stewed mulberries and blackberries are a wonderful autumnal dessert served with a ginger and rose-flavoured cream. Mulberry trees are bursting with berries during early summer in the Kalash valley of Chitral, home to the ancient tribes people of Kalash who are said to be descendants of Alexander the Great's army. You can see their gorgeous children, wearing traditional dress, shaking the branches and catching the fruit on large sheets below, before indulging in their haul.

200g/7 oz dried black
  mulberries
300g/2¼ cup/10½ oz
  blackberries
150g/¾ cup/5½ oz
  cherries, pitted
½ tsp ground ginger
about 250ml/9 fl oz/
  generous 1 cup water
3 tbsp honey

To serve
handful of walnuts, roughly
  chopped
200ml/7 fl oz/scant 1
  cup thick double (heavy)
  cream whipped and
  flavoured with
  ginger and rose water

Preparation 15 minutes | **Cooking** 30 minutes | **Serves** 5–6

Bring the mulberries, blackberries, cherries, ginger and water to the boil in a saucepan. Turn the heat down and simmer for 20 minutes, adding water as you need, to keep the berries covered.

After about 20 minutes, add the honey, stir and take the pan off the heat. Allow to cool in the pan.

Serve with chopped walnuts and the flavoured whipped cream either at room temperature, or chill in the fridge until later.

Pomegranate, rose and cardamom halva jelly

This is more of a jelly-like dessert than a traditional halva, but it is inspired by the flourishing pomegranate trees that grow in areas of Pakistan – those lush green leaves that hide away a shiny fruit heavy with jewel-like seeds. This dish is best served in small pretty glasses, decorated with gold leaf, either as a light finish to a heavy meal, or a palate cleanser between courses.

5 pomegranates, seeds only
250ml/9 fl oz/generous
   1 cup water
2 cardamom pods, seeds
   removed and finely ground
120g/4¼ oz/⅔ cup caster
   (superfine) sugar
1 tsp agar agar powder
1 tsp rose water or kewra
   (screwpine extract)

To decorate
gold leaf
pomegranate seeds

Preparation 40 minutes + chilling | **Cooking** 10 minutes | **Serves** 4–6

Blitz the pomegranate seeds in a blender or juicer, then pour it through a sieve to remove the seeds.

Pour the juice into a bowl, allow to settle, then add the water, finely ground cardamom and sugar. Pour the mixture into a saucepan and heat gently. Do not let the juice come to the boil, keep it on a simmer, and slowly add the agar agar, stirring until dissolved.

Add the rose water or kewra and turn off the heat. Allow to cool for 2 minutes so it doesn't crack the serving glasses. (Agar-based jelly can set without refrigeration so don't leave it any longer.) Pour the jelly into glasses and chill in the fridge for around 30 minutes, until set.

To serve, decorate with gold leaf and pomegranate seeds.

Fresh curd burutz cheese

with walnuts, apricots, figs and honey

This dish is a memory of mountain hospitality – a platter filled with fresh fruit from the garden, nuts dried from the season before and homemade curd cheese from cow's milk. Traditionally made in Hunza, burutz cheese is a buttermilk-based cheese where buttermilk is bashed about in the dried sheep belly skin until the fat separates and forms a thick cheese. This is a quicker way of making it with Greek yogurt. Serve either after dinner, as an afternoon teatime snack or as part of a light lunch.

For the cheese
400g/14 oz/1¾ cups Greek yogurt
a pinch of salt
honey, to serve

For the fruit platter, a selection of:
fresh figs, grapes, apricots or greengages
dried apricots
dried figs
raisins
walnuts
pistachios

Preparation 20 minutes + overnight standing | **Serves** 6–8

To make the cheese, place a piece of muslin cloth in a colander over the sink. Mix the yogurt and salt together in a bowl until combined.

Pour the yogurt into the muslin cloth, then bring the corners of the cloth together, tie into a knot and hang over the tap overnight to let all the whey drip into the sink.

In the morning it should be a soft cheese. Serve with fruits and nuts or store in an airtight container in the fridge for 1–2 days.

Pakwan

Wheat flour and jaggery rolls with aniseed

Eaten as an afternoon snack in the north, pakwan is a healthy small round bread, which is made with wholemeal flour, jaggery and aniseed. The mouth-watering aromas of this bread cooking on a tawa, the smokines from a wood burner and the smell of cardamom green tea slowly simmering on the stove is relived when I make these in my kitchen at home.

150g/5½ oz/1 cup wholemeal (wholewheat) flour, plus extra for dusting
2 tbsp fine semolina
150g/5½ oz/generous 1 cup jaggery or muscovado sugar, plus 2 tbsp for melting
3–4 cardamom pods, seeds removed and ground
1 tsp ground aniseed
2 tbsp desiccated (dry unsweetened) coconut
1 tbsp poppy seeds
1 egg, beaten
milk for kneading
300ml/10 fl oz/1¼ cups vegetable oil or ghee, for frying

Preparation 20 minutes | **Cooking** 15 minutes | **Serves** 7–8

Place all the ingredients, except the 2 tablespoons of jaggery for melting and oil for frying, in a bowl and knead into a soft dough using enough milk to bind it together.

Heat the oil for frying in a wok over a medium heat. Roll out the dough on a lightly floured work surface until it is 5mm/¼ inch thick. Using a 2cm/¾-inch round pastry cutter, cut out 7–8 circles and carefully drop them into the hot oil in batches. Deep-fry for 2–3 minutes on each side until golden brown. Remove with a slotted spoon and drain on kitchen paper.

Melt the reserved 2 tablespoons of jaggery in a pan and drizzle over the pakwan. Eat warm.

Gajar mukhadi

Semolina and carrot pudding

I was taught this recipe from a Pathan lady, who incorporated two of my favourite dessert ingredients – carrots and semolina – in this Pathan/Punjabi pudding. However, this is one of those recipes that is usually served with a variety of savoury barbecue dishes.

160g/5¾ oz/1 cup fine
  semolina
3 tbsp ghee
3 cardamom pods, seeds
  removed and finely ground
120g/4¼ oz/⅔ cup caster
  (superfine) sugar
6 carrots, finely grated

To serve (optional)
chopped pistachios
khoya / milk fudge
  (see p23)

Preparation 10 minutes + 20 minutes soaking | **Cooking** 25 minutes | **Serves** 4–5

Soak the semolina in a bowl of cold water for 20 minutes, then drain.

Heat the ghee in a heavy-based saucepan over a medium heat, add the ground cardamom and sugar and allow the sugar to dissolve.

Add the soaked semolina and cook for 5–6 minutes. Add the grated carrots and start to stir vigorously. Continue cooking for another 6–8 minutes until the halva comes together, the ghee separates out and the mixture comes away from the side of the pan.

Serve hot with chopped pistachios and khoya, if you like.

A saffron blaze
Following the spice caravans

Spices are the fabric of flavour and Pakistani food is bare without them. When making desserts I find myself particularly drawn to saffron. The very sight of it conjures up a vision of autumn fields ablaze with amethyst-coloured crocus flowers that carpet the ground for a few short weeks, then wilt away and disappear as if they were a dream. Linked with a romanticism that has stirred emperors and common folk alike to conquer and barter, their three crimson-hued stigmas are worth their weight in gold.

The ubiquitous rose, cardamom and saffron that now perfume Pakistani cuisine were introduced by people invading and migrating from Iran and Afghanistan. The use of these flavours in Pakistani and Afghani bakeries have created some of my sweetest food memories.

There was something distinctive about cakes and biscuits from my local Afghani bakery. The bakery itself was always inviting, with the intense heat from the ovens, the air strongly scented with cardamom and pastry dough, and the counters packed with Iranian flatbreads, cream and pineapple cakes, and baskets of sweet or savoury biscuits. Heady saffron-infused baklava-style pastries and sesame brittle are still some of my favourite treats.

The flavours of this chapter are inspired by those gleeful childhood visits to Afghani and Irani bakeries, whose sweets filled my childhood with exotic flavours and the image of fields of crocus flowers.

Afghani gosh-e-fil

Elephant ear-shaped fried pastry with ground pistachio and cardamom

As a child I would love the idea of nibbling on pastries with such a sweet name. 'Gosh e fil' in Persian means elephant ears, which is what these simple pastries resemble. The delicious flavours come from kneading with cardamom, then dusting with icing sugar, finely ground pistachios and rose petals.

220g/7¾ oz/1⅔ cups plain (all-purpose) flour, plus extra 30g/1 oz for kneading and extra for dusting
a pinch of salt
1 tbsp caster (superfine) sugar
3–4 cardamom pods, seeds removed and ground
2 eggs
40g/1½ oz/3 tbsp unsalted butter, melted and cooled
4 tbsp whole milk
vegetable oil, for frying

To decorate
1 tbsp icing (confectioners') sugar
1 tbsp ground pistachio
1 tsp pink dried rose petals

Preparation 20 minutes + 1 hour resting | **Cooking** 20 minutes | **Makes** 15–20

Sift the flour, salt, sugar and ground cardamom together in a large bowl.

Whisk the eggs, butter and milk together in another bowl, then pour this slowly into the flour and start to bring it together into a dough. When it begins to combine and is sticky, place it on a floured surface. Using the extra 30g/1oz of flour knead for about 10 minutes until you have a soft dough. Cover the dough with a damp tea towel and allow to rest for 1 hour at room temperature.

When ready to cook, roll the dough out on a floured surface into a thin sheet about 5mm/¼ inch thick, then using a 5cm/2-inch round pastry cutter, cut out 15–20 circles. Using your fingers, form the circles into an 'ear' shape with a little point at one end.

Heat the oil in a wok-like pan to 180°C/350°F, or until a cube of bread browns in 30 seconds. Drop a few 'ears' into the hot oil over a medium heat, allow them to float to the top and deep-fry until light brown and crispy. Remove with a slotted spoon and drain on kitchen paper. Repeat untill all the 'ears' are cooked.

Allow to cool, then dust with icing sugar and sprinkle with finely ground pistachios and rose petals. Store in an airtight jar for 1 week.

Afghani asabia el aroos

Pine nut, pistachio and almond filled filo pastry soaked
in rose water syrup

*These cigar-shaped filo pastries, filled with mixed nuts and soaked in sweet rose
water sugar syrup, are based on baklava. They remind me of the ones I used to
buy with my pocket money from Afghani bakeries in Karachi, as they would make
such a change from typical Pakistani mithai (sweetmeats).*

For the filling
150g/5½ oz/1½ cups mixed
    ground pistachios, almonds
    and pine nuts, plus 1
    tbsp ground pistachios,
    to decorate
40g/1½ oz/¼ cup caster
    (superfine) sugar, plus
    extra for sprinkling
½ tsp ground cinnamon
2 cardamom pods, seeds
    removed and ground

For the sugar syrup
140g/5 oz/¾ cup caster
    (superfine) sugar
300ml/10 fl oz/1¼ cups
    water
1 tsp lemon juice
3 tbsp honey
1 tsp rose water

For the pastry
350g/12 oz filo (phyllo)
    pastry
50g/1¾ oz/3½ tbsp unsalted
    butter, melted and cooled,
    plus extra for greasing
1 egg yolk
2 tbsp water

Preparation 30 minutes | **Cooking** 30–35 minutes | **Makes** 8–10

Mix all the filling ingredients together in a small bowl and set aside.

To make the sugar syrup bring the sugar and water to the boil in a saucepan.
Turn the heat down and simmer for 15–20 minutes until it is a thick syrup
at the single thread stage (see p22). Turn off the heat and add the lemon.
Once the syrup is a little cooler, stir in the honey and rose water. Set aside.

Now prepare the pastry. Cut the filo in half, then in half again to create
10cm/4-inch wide and 30cm/12-inch long strips. Stack them up and cover
them with a damp tea towel to prevent the dough from drying out.

Place 2 filo rectangles on the work surface with the shorter sides facing you,
and brush the top of one with some of the melted butter, then top it with
the other. There's no need to brush the second one with butter.

Place 1 tablespoon of the filling in a line across the shorter side of the filo
that faces you. Fold in the longer edges of the pastry, sealing in the sides of
the filling. Roll the pastry up from the short side, forming a fat cigar shape.
Place on the baking sheet with the visible edge facing down. Repeat.

Cover the cigars with a wet cloth to prevent them drying out. When ready
to bake, preheat the oven to 180°C/350°F/gas mark 4 and grease a baking
tray. Place the cigars on the prepared baking tray, brush the tops with a
mixture of egg yolk and water, sprinkle with caster sugar and bake in the
oven for 12–15 minutes, or until the tops are light golden.

As soon as the filo cigars come out of the oven, using a pair of tongs, dip each cigar into the sugar syrup and let them absorb the liquid for 1–2 minutes, then remove. Serve at room temperature, pouring a little of the syrup over the cigars and sprinkling with ground pistachios to decorate.

Badami kulcha

Almond and cardamom meringues

These Afghani meringues are just a delight to make and eat. I remember walking into my local Afghani bakery at the weekend and, after paying with my pocket money, being handed a small brown paper bag filled with these clouds of sweet indulgence. The cardamom has a delicate, sweet yet powerful aroma, which comes alive with each bite.

375g/13 oz/2½ cups ground almonds
100g/3½ oz/¾ cup plain (all-purpose) white flour
3–4 cardamom pods, seeds removed and ground
4 egg whites
¼ tsp cream of tartar
275g/9¾ oz/2 cups icing (confectioners') sugar, plus extra for rolling biscuits and dusting
10–12 whole blanched almonds, to decorate

Preparation 20 minutes | **Cooking** 30 minutes | **Makes** 10–12

Preheat the oven to 180°C/350°F/gas mark 4. Prepare a tray lined with non-stick baking sheet.

Mix the ground almonds, flour and ground cardamom together in a bowl. Set aside.

Whisk the egg whites in another bowl until foamy, then add the cream of tartar and beat until soft peaks form. Gradually add the icing sugar and beat until stiff peaks form. Slowly and gently fold in the ground almonds mixture with a rubber spatula, and don't over-mix.

Dust a clean surface or plate with icing sugar. Lightly dust your hands with icing sugar, then scoop out 1 tablespoon of the mixture and form it into a ball with your hands. Roll the ball gently in the icing sugar and place it on the baking sheet. Repeat until you have used up all of the mixture.

Lightly press a whole blanched almond in the middle of each biscuit without flattening it, and bake in the oven for about 30 minutes until the biscuit is light brown around the edges.

Take out of the oven and allow to cool, then dust the tops with icing sugar. Store in an airtight container for up to 1 week.

Sesame gajak

Sesame seed and jaggery melt-in-the-mouth snaps

Chickie (brittle) and gajak sweets are always on counters of bakeries, sweet shops and stalls in Pakistan. These crisp sesame seed sweets with jaggery syrup are a childhood treat and I bought them mostly from dried fruit stalls owned by Pathans, but I also found them in my corner bakery. They are a comforting flavour of home.

150g/5½ oz/1 cup sesame seeds
1 tbsp ghee, for greasing
150g/5½ oz/generous 1 cup jaggery or muscovado sugar
a pinch of salt
120ml/4 fl oz/½ cup water
3–4 cardamom pods, seeds removed and ground

Preparation 20 minutes | **Cooking** 25 minutes | **Serves** 5–6

Dry-roast the sesame seeds in a frying pan for 30 seconds–1 minute, then place them on a sheet of parchment paper and allow to cool. Grease another sheet of parchment paper with ghee and set aside on a baking tray.

Heat the jaggery, salt and water in a saucepan to 116°C/240°F without stirring. Add the sesame seeds and ground cardamom and stir to combine, then turn off the heat and allow the mixture to cool to 43°C/110°F. Once cooled, mix vigorously with a wooden spoon to thicken.

Pour the mixture on to the prepared parchment paper and spread it out until it is 1cm/½ inch thick. Allow to cool completely.

Break the brittle into rough bite-sized pieces and store in an airtight container for 2–3 days.

Khanfaroush

Spiced saffron crumpets with honey

This is an Emirati-inspired recipe I picked up on my travels. These are best described as a cross between crumpets and pancake-style cakes. Even though they weren't a usual at my Afghani bakery, their flavour reminds me of the floral intensity of sweets and cakes from my childhood.

a pinch of saffron threads
1 tbsp hot water
1 tbsp rose water
4 large eggs, lightly beaten
120g/4¼ oz/scant 1 cup rice flour
75g/2¾ oz/9 tbsp plain (all-purpose) flour
1 tsp baking powder
50g/1¾ oz/¼ cup caster (superfine) sugar
3–4 cardamom pods, seeds removed and ground
sunflower oil, for frying

To decorate
1 tbsp icing (confectioners') sugar
honey, for drizzling
1 tbsp slivered pistachios

Preparation 20 minutes + 15 minutes soaking + 20 minutes resting
Cooking 35 minutes | **Makes** 9–10

Soak the saffron in the hot water for 15 minutes.

Combine the rose water and saffron with the lightly beaten eggs in a bowl and set aside.

Mix all the dry ingredients together in another bowl. Make a well in the middle, pour in the egg mixture and begin whisking until it is a thick batter. Cover with clingfilm or a tea towel and allow to rest for about 20 minutes.

Using a heavy-based cast-iron frying pan or pancake pan, heat a little oil over a medium heat. Place 1 large tablespoon of the batter in the pan and cook for about 2–3 minutes on each side until golden brown. Remove and drain on kitchen paper. Keep warm in a foil pouch. Repeat in batches until all the batter is used up.

Dust the crumpets with icing sugar, drizzle with honey, then sprinkle with pistachios and serve hot.

Saffron and cashew bal mithai

Caramelised cashew sweets with sugar nibs

I always found this sweet the most attractive in bakeries – rectangular toffee-coloured sweets covered in sugar nibs. Traditionally, khoya (see p23) is cooked down with cane sugar until it turns brown, which is then colloquially called 'chocolate' even though there isn't any cocoa in it. I have changed the recipe and used condensed milk with ground cashews, which I cooked until brown.

2 tbsp ghee
3–4 cardamom pods, seeds removed and ground
250g/9 oz/2 cups cashews, ground
150–200ml/5–7 fl oz/⅔– scant 1 cup condensed milk
a pinch of saffron threads
3 tbsp white sugar nibs

Preparation 15 minutes | **Cooking** 20 minutes | **Makes** 8–10

Heat the ghee in a heavy-based saucepan, add the ground cardamom and ground cashews and stir for 7–10 minutes until fragrant. Add the condensed milk and begin to stir vigorously. Add the saffron and keep stirring for about 6–8 minutes. As soon as the mixture comes together like a ball and it is a medium–dark brown colour and shiny, take the pan off the heat and allow to cool in the pan.

Spread the sugar nibs out in a dish. Using your hands, divide the mixture into 8–10 golf ball-sized portions, then shape them into small rectangular pieces. Roll in the sugar nibs and place in a serving dish.

Serve immediately or store in the fridge for up to 3 days but eat at room temperature.

Nan-e nokhochi

Chickpea flour shortbread with cloves

This Parsi/Iranian biscuit recipe made with chickpea flour found its way into my home through my maths tutor. I hated going to my tutor's house (because of the maths), but I always went because after the lesson I got to chat with other pupils while nibbling on these delicate biscuits flavoured with cloves.

200g/7 oz/¾ cup plus 2 tbsp unsalted butter, melted, plus extra for greasing
250g/9 oz/scant 1½ cups caster (superfine) sugar
3–4 cardamom pods, seeds removed and finely ground
½ tsp ground cloves
1 tsp rose water
350g/12 oz/scant 3 cups chickpea (gram) flour, plus extra for dusting
1 tbsp slivered pistachios

Preparation 20 minutes + 1 hour chilling | **Cooking** 25 minutes | **Makes** 10–12

Combine the melted butter, sugar, cardamom, cloves and rose water in a bowl and beat with a spoon until smooth, white and creamy. Add the chickpea flour and mix for 1 minute until the dough is no longer sticky.

Dust a clean work surface with chickpea flour and knead the dough for about 2–3 minutes. Flatten the dough with your hand until it is about 2cm/¾ inch thick, then wrap in clingfilm and chill in the fridge for 1 hour.

Preheat the oven to 150°C/300°F/gas mark 2 and grease a baking tray.

Unwrap the dough on a work surface. Using a 4cm/1½-inch flower or 4-petal biscuit cutter, cut out 10–12 biscuits and place on the prepared baking tray, spacing them at least 2.5cm/1 inch apart to allow them to expand during cooking.

Press 1–2 slivers of pistachio on top and bake in the oven for about 20–25 minutes, or until golden. Allow to cool on a wire rack and store in an airtight container for 10 days.

Peshawari pistachio ice cream

As a late-night, after-dinner indulgence my father would treat us to Peshawari ice cream. Made in a large stainless-steel tubs, it had an intense hit of pistachio essence, which was sublime with the texture of the whole nuts and the buffalo milk cream. If the bakery next door was open we would always get a few biscuits to dunk in the melted ice cream.

500ml/17 fl oz/2 cups whole unpasteurised milk
100g/3½ oz/½ cup caster (superfine) sugar
1 tbsp cornflour (cornstarch)
1 tsp Arabic mastic crystals
500ml/17 fl oz/2 cups double (heavy) cream
40g/1½ oz/⅓ cup whole shelled unsalted pistachios, chopped
½ tsp pistachio essence (optional)
½ tsp vanilla extract
1 tsp kewra (screwpine extract)
1 tsp gelatine powder

Preparation 15 minutes + 5 hours freezing | **Cooking** 10 minutes | **Serves** 6–8

Begin by heating the milk in a heavy-based saucepan. When it starts to boil, turn the heat down, add the sugar and let it dissolve.

Mix the cornflour and a little water together in a small bowl to make a paste. Crush the mastic crystals in a mortar and pestle, add to the milk and stir, then gradually add the cornflour mixture to the simmering milk and stir until it begins to thicken slightly. Turn off the heat and allow to cool for 5 minutes. Now stir in the remaining ingredients. Cover and allow to cool completely.

Transfer the mixture to an ice-cream machine and churn according to the manufacturer's instructions.

If you don't have an ice-cream machine, pour into a metallic bowl, cover and place in the freezer for 1 hour. Take out of the freezer and using a whisk, whisk the mixture then freeze again for another hour. Whisk one more time, then place the container in a ziplock bag and freeze for 2–3 hours before serving. This makes sure that the ice cream stays soft.

Badami zafran halva ladoo
Ground almond and saffron balls

You can't escape ladoos of any kind in Pakistan, be it semolina, chickpea flour or wheat – and this chapter wouldn't be complete without them. Many bakeries in Pakistan have a mithai (sweetmeat) corner as Pakistanis and their sweet tooth wouldn't go far without a ladoo. I love these, as they melt in your mouth.

150g/5½ oz/generous 1 cup blanched almonds
2 pinches of saffron threads
2 tbsp ghee
200ml/7 fl oz/scant 1 cup condensed milk
2–3 tbsp desiccated (dry unsweetened) coconut, plus 2 tbsp for rolling
50g/1¾ oz khoya / milk fudge (see p23)

Preparation 40 minutes + overnight soaking | **Cooking** 20 minutes | **Makes** 10–12

Place the almonds in a heatproof bowl and pour in enough hot water to cover. Allow to soak overnight.

The next day, soak the saffron in a little hot water for 15–20 minutes.

Drain the soaked almonds, and using about 2–3 tablespoons of the saffron water, grind the almonds to a paste in a food processor.

Heat the ghee in a heavy-based saucepan over a medium heat. When hot, add the ground almond paste and fry for 3–4 minutes stirring constantly. Add the condensed milk and coconut and stir until the mixture comes together and forms a shiny ball in the saucepan. Turn off the heat and allow to cool in the pan for 10 minutes.

Using your hands, shape the mixture into 10–12 golf ball-sized balls, then roll them in some khoya (just a little will stick to the surface) and coconut.

Serve immediately or store, covered, in the fridge for 1–2 days. Best eaten at room temperature.

Afghani awb-e-dundawn

Rose water biscuits

I called these biscuits 'rose water melts' when I was growing up. This is an adaptation of a classic Afghani biscuit, which I found in a bakery near my home, and it has always been my quick nostalgia fix.

180g/6 oz/1⅓ cups plain (all-purpose) flour
115g/4 oz/scant ⅔ cup caster (superfine) sugar
3–4 cardamom pods, seeds removed and ground
2–3 tbsp melted ghee, plus extra for greasing
2 tsp rose water
60ml/2 fl oz/¼ cup whole milk
3 tbsp ground pistachios, to decorate

Preparation 20 minutes | **Cooking** 15–20 minutes | **Makes** 10–12

Preheat the oven 180°C/350°F/gas mark 4 and grease a baking tray.

Sift the flour into a large bowl, then add the sugar, cardamo, melted ghee and rose water and mix together. Add the milk and mix to make a soft dough.

Using your hands, divide the dough into 5cm/2-inch balls and place on the prepared baking tray, about 5cm/2 inches apart.

Bake in the oven for 15–20 minutes, then remove from the oven and immediately sprinkle with the ground pistachios. Allow to cool on a wire rack. Store in an airtight container for 1 week.

Festive spice and roses
Celebratory sweets

Being given a mithai (sweetmeat) box heavy with the weight of its contents as a gift always filled my childish heart with sweet anticipation. This treat would be a box of celebratory sweets announcing a happy occasion and its significance goes to the very heart of Pakistani culture. A child is born, a union blessed – nothing goes unsweetened.

At weddings, large baskets decorated with roses and brimming with silver leaf-decorated mithai are given as gifts between the families and trays adorned with cardamom-scented ladoos are fed to the bride and groom by well-wishers as an act of welcoming a new family member. On Eid, sheer khurma infused with saffron and rich dried fruit is offered as a welcoming drink to guests, and on passing exams parents shower friends and family kewra-laced gulab jamuns and barfi.

Festive desserts are a labour of love, heavy with spice, and watching them being cooked is a sight to savour. Massive stainless-steel cooking pots are constantly stirred as they are filled with milk slow-cooked to a clotted cream consistency, then sweet fruits or vegetables with kilos of sugar are added and exotically spiced with saffron, kewra, cardamom or cloves. Hours are spent making sweets or pouring out individually decorated servings. The happier the occasion, the sweeter the offering.

In Pakistan, no dawwat (feast) can be without a large platter of decadent desserts, perfumed mithais or halvas – this practice is engrained in Pakistani cultural hospitality as a way of sharing joy with loved ones.

Gajar ka halva

Carrot halva served with whipped cream

Carrots in Pakistan are deep red, sweet and intensely crunchy. They are a winter vegetable, so this dessert is a favourite at wedding dinners during cooler months. Many families have their own secret recipe for gajar ka halva that goes back generations. This one is my Dadi's (paternal grandmother) and has been adapted by my mother. The slow cooking intensifies the infusion of cloves and saffron, which combines with the intensity of the sweet carrots as this halva bubbles away to a rich, shiny fruition. This is the ultimate Pakistani celebration dessert.

100ml/3½ fl oz/scant ½ cup whole milk
400ml/14 fl oz/1¾ cups double (heavy) cream
500g/1 lb 2 oz/3¾ cups carrots, grated
5–6 cloves
5 cardamom pods, seeds removed
100g/3½ oz/½ cup caster (superfine) sugar
a generous pinch of saffron threads
2 tbsp desiccated (dry unsweetened) coconut
1 tbsp roughly ground pistachios
natural red food colour (optional)
whipped cream or vanilla ice cream, to serve

To decorate
1 tbsp raisins
1 tbsp flaked (slivered) almonds
1 tbsp slivered pistachios
2 sheets gold leaf

Preparation 25 minutes | **Cooking** 1 hour | **Serves** 6–8

Bring the milk and cream to the boil in a heavy-based saucepan, add the grated carrots, cloves and cardamom seeds and cook over a medium–low heat, stirring occasionally, for about 25–30 minutes until the milk and cream are absorbed into the carrot. Keep an eye on the it in case it starts to burn or stick on the base of the pan.

Now add the sugar and saffron, keep stirring until it is thoroughly mixed in. Stir in the coconut and ground pistachios.

Once the halva is thick and deep red (you can add a little red food colour if the carrots are a bit pale) and all the cream/milk and sugar is absorbed, pour it into a serving dish and decorate with raisins, almonds, pistachios and gold leaf. Serve warm or cold with whipped cream or ice cream.

Balushahi
Festive glazed curd doughnut

These flaky pastry-like doughnuts are fried and then dunked into a spiced sugar syrup. They are always the best surprise in celebratory mithai (sweetmeat) boxes. Although these are traditionally flavoured with saffron, I have created an unusual mix of turmeric, black cardamom and vanilla for the syrup in this recipe.

For the doughnuts
200g/7 oz/1½ cups plain (all-purpose) flour
¼ tsp salt
¼ tsp bicarbonate of soda (baking soda)
60g/2¼ oz/¼ cup ghee
6 tbsp whole plain chilled yogurt
vegetable oil, for deep-frying

For the sugar syrup
240ml/8 fl oz/1 cup water
375g/13 oz/2 cups caster (superfine) sugar
¼ tsp ground turmeric
1 black cardamom pod
½ tsp vanilla extract
2 tsp lemon juice

To decorate
2 tbsp white poppy seeds

Preparation 25 minutes + 45 minutes resting | **Cooking** 25 minutes | **Makes** 10–12

First, make the doughnuts. Put the flour, salt and bicarbonate of soda into a large bowl and stir to combine. Next, add the ghee and, using your fingers, mix together until it resembles coarse crumbs. It takes a good 1 minute to get this texture. Add the yogurt and knead just enough until all the ingredients come together. Cover the dough with a wet muslin cloth and allow to rest for about 30 minutes at room temperature.

Divide the dough into 10–12 equal portions, the size of large lemons, and make a dent in the centre of each with your thumb. Try not to press too much while shaping them as this can cause them to crack. Cover the dough portions with a wet cloth and allow them to rest for another 15 minutes at room temperature.

Heat the oil for deep-frying in a deep saucepan to 180°C/350°F, or until a cube of bread browns in 30 seconds. Once the oil is hot, start adding a few balls at a time into the oil and fry them over a medium heat. The medium heat helps the balushahi to cook evenly from the inside. As soon as the dough balls float to the surface, flip them over and fry until the bottom half is dark golden brown. Once both sides are well browned, remove with a slotted spoon and drain on kitchen paper. Continue with the rest of the dough balls.

For the sugar syrup, heat the water, sugar, turmeric, black cardamom pod and vanilla together in a saucepan over a medium heat, stirring well until the sugar dissolves and the mixture comes to the boil.

Turn the heat to low and simmer until it is at the double thread stage (see p22). Then add the lemon juice to stop the syrup crystallising.

Dip the fried doughnuts, one at a time, into the sugar syrup, making sure they are coated all over and arange them on a serving platter. Decorate the balushahi with white poppy seeds and allow to rest until the sugar hardens.

Shahi tukra brioche bread pudding

with saffron, ricotta, cranberries and chopped nuts

This is a festive bread pudding with a history that goes as far back as the Mughal emperors, but I have updated it by using sweet brioche bread to add a rich flavour. This dessert can either be baked or unbaked and served chilled or warm.

1 litre/1¾ pints/4 cups whole milk
250ml/9 fl oz/generous 1 cup condensed milk
a pinch of saffron threads
4 cardamom pods, seeds removed and finely crushed
150g/5½ oz/⅔ cup ricotta
3 tbsp ghee or unsalted butter
10 slices of brioche loaf, cut in half
handful of chopped pistachios, almonds, pine nuts, dried cranberries, cherries and raisins
dried rose petals
gold or silver leaf

Preparation 25 minutes + chilling | **Cooking** 30 minutes | **Serves** 6–8

Put the milk, condensed milk, saffron and cardamom together in a heavy-based pan and bring to the boil over a low–medium heat. Turn the heat down to low, add the ricotta, stir until smooth (tiny lumps may remain, which are fine) and cook for 10 minutes until thick. Take the pan off the heat and set aside.

Heat 1 teaspoon of the ghee in a pan, add a brioche slice and fry until it is toasted on both sides. Transfer the brioche to an ovenproof dish and repeat frying all each slice of brioche in 1 teaspoon of ghee.

Pour the milk mixture over the brioche and decorate with nuts, berries and raisins. At this point you can either refrigerate or bake in an oven preheated to 180°C/350°F/gas mark 4 for 15–20 minutes until golden brown.

Scatter rose petals over the top and adorn with gold or silver leaf to serve.

Rose lab-e-shireen

Pakistani trifle with lychee, mango, cardamom milk and vermicelli

This eye-catching dessert is made in large stainless-steel platters and sold by the kilo. It is a hotchpotch of Pakistani sweet flavours – seasonal fruit, rose, cardamom, jelly, sweet vermicelli and Rooh Afza rose syrup. Its vibrant colours and its many textures are captivating. A Karachi favourite with Arab roots, it is a great celebratory dessert.

2 packets of 2 different flavoured jelly crystals
500ml/17 fl oz/2 cups whole milk
2–3 cardamom pods, seeds removed and finely crushed
a handful of plain or coloured vermicelli
150ml/5 fl oz/⅔ cup ready-made custard
1 mango, roughly chopped
6–8 canned or fresh lychees
2–3 tbsp rose syrup

To decorate
2 tbsp chopped pistachios
1 tbsp roasted blanched almonds
1 tbsp dried rose petals

Preparation 20 minutes + 2 hours chilling | **Cooking** 10 minutes | **Serves** 6–8

Begin by preparing the jelly according to the packet instructions and chill in the fridge for 2 hours, or until set. Remove the jelly and cut into icecube-sized squares. Place in the fridge.

Next, make the cardamom milk. Bring the milk and cardamom to the boil in a saucepan. As soon as it is boiling, turn off the heat, allow to cool, then transfer to the fridge.

Cook the vermicelli in a saucepan of boiling salted water for 5–8 minutes until soft, then drain and set aside.

When ready to assemble the dish, begin by placing the cooked vermicelli at the base of a large glass serving bowl. Next, add the jelly cubes, then the ready-made custard, then pour over the cardamom milk and top with some of the fruit pieces. Drizzle with the rose syrup and swirl it so that it colours the milk pink, then decorate with chopped pistachios, almonds, rose petals and the remaining fruit. Serve chilled.

Meva naan

Sweet bread with dried fruit

A sweet celebration naan bread, which is delicious dipped in a cup of chai after a long, spicy festive meal. Serve them as soon as they are cooked.

For the naan

320g/11¼ oz/2¼ cups strong plain (all purpose) flour, plus extra for dusting
1 tsp baking powder
¼ tsp bicarbonate of soda (baking soda)
a pinch of salt
2 tsp soft brown sugar
1 egg, beaten
2 tbsp ghee, plus extra for coating and brushing
100ml/3½ fl oz/scant ½ cup whole plain yogurt, beaten
150ml/5 fl oz/⅔ cup whole milk, or as needed during kneading
choice of seeds, spices, fresh herbs and dried fruit, for sprinkling

Preparation 30 minutes + 1–3 hours rising | **Cooking** 15 minutes | **Makes** 7–8

Sift the flour, baking powder, bicarbonate of soda, salt and sugar together into a large bowl. Make a well in the middle and pour in the beaten egg and ghee and, using your hands, work the dough into a ball. Add the yogurt and the milk (you may need a little more) and knead until it is a smooth dough. (If using a stand mixer, place all the dry ingredients, egg and yogurt in the bowl and pour the milk in gradually while the mixer kneads with a dough hook. Knead until a dough is formed.)

Coat the dough lightly with a little ghee, then cover with a damp tea towel and allow to rise in a warm place for at least 1 hour, or up to a maximum of 3 hours. The dough should have risen, but not quite doubled in size.

Knead the dough again briefly on a lightly floured surface, then divide it into 7–8 small round balls. Using a rolling pin, roll the dough into an oblong naan shape with tapering ends, then pierce all over with a fork. Brush the naans lightly with ghee and sprinkle over your choice of seeds, spices, fresh herbs and dried fruit.

Preheat the oven to 200°C/400°F/gas mark 6 or preheat the grill to high. Heat a dry heavy-based non-stick frying pan over a medium heat. When hot, slap on the naan and cook gently until it is lightly browned on the bottom, then transfer the naans to a baking tray and slide onto the shelf of the hot oven or grill. Cook the naans for 4–5 minutes, or until they rise and little brown air pockets form on the top. Serve.

Saffron-infused zarda

Sweet rice with nuts, coconut, candied fruit and khoya

Glistening in shades of tangerine and pale rust, sweet saffron rice can be a festive dessert, a teatime snack and sometimes an accompaniment to savoury dishes, or eaten as an appetiser.

a large pinch of saffron
   threads
1 tsp hot water
8–10 cloves
5–7 cardamom pods
275g/9¼ oz/1⅔ cups
   basmati rice
2 tbsp ghee
350ml/12 fl oz /1½ cups
   water
300g/10½ oz/1⅓ cups
   caster (superfine) sugar
1 tbsp pistachios
1 tbsp pine nuts
½ tbsp chopped candied
   peel or candied papaya

To decorate
1 tbsp glacé (candied)
   cherries, chopped
1 tbsp desiccated (dry
   unsweetened) coconut
4 tbsp khoya / milk fudge
   (see p23)

Preparation 10 minutes + 30 minutes soaking | **Cooking** 30 minutes | **Serves** 4–6

Soak the saffron in the hot water for 30 minutes. Fill a saucepan with enough water for cooking the rice, then add 3–4 cloves and 3 cardamom pods and bring to the boil. Add the rice and par-cook for 2 minutes, then drain and set aside.

Heat the ghee in a dry saucepan, add the remaining cloves and cardamom pods, the measured water and sugar, and make into an single thread syrup (see p22).

Add the par-cooked rice and nuts, and stir. The water should just about cover the rice. Cover the saucepan with a lid and turn the heat down to low. Check every 5 minutes, stir gently and cover again. Keep doing this until the rice is nearly cooked through.

Once the rice is nearly done, pour in the saffron, keep the heat on low and cook, covered, for a few more minutes. The rice should be completely cooked through but not over-soft or mushy.

Serve in a bowl topped with candied peel, glacé cherries, desiccated coconut and khoya.

Qawwami seviyan
Roasted vermicelli topped with nuts

Eid is a time of celebration and enjoying all things decadent. Seviyan is a quintessential Pakistani Eid dessert, which is served as a welcoming sweetness to guests visiting on the day. Every family has their own recipe and this is one that has been in my father's side of the family for generations. Qawwami seviyan is a sugar preserved roasted vermicelli dessert that's eaten with cream or milk. My Dadi (paternal grandmother) would make it traditionally with one part seviyan to 16 parts sugar, but now my mother makes it with less sugar. Served best with malai clotted cream (see p23).

a pinch of saffron threads
1 tbsp hot milk
4–5 tbsp ghee
4–5 cardamom pods
5–6 cloves
150g/5½ oz/1 cup broken dry seviyan (vermicelli)
350g/12 oz/2 cups caster (superfine) sugar
175ml/6 fl oz/¾ cup water
1 litre/1¾ pints/4 cups whole milk
ice-cold or warm milk or cream, to serve

To decorate
3 tbsp flaked (slivered) almonds
3 tbsp slivered pistachios
2 tbsp sultanas (golden raisins)
sliver or gold leaf, or rose petals (optional)

Preparation 15 minutes + 20 minutes soaking | **Cooking** 1 hour | **Serves** 8–10

Soak the saffron in the hot milk for 20 minutes.

Heat the ghee in a small frying pan over a medium heat, add the cardamom pods and cloves and fry until fragrant. Once the aroma develops, add the seviyan and fry, stirring to make sure that the seviyan does not burn but slowly turns a light brown colour. You might have to keep moving the pan off the heat and stirring to make sure it doesn't burn.

In another pan, heat the sugar and water together until the sugar has dissolved and you have a single thread syrup (see p22). Add the fried seviyan to the sugar syrup and mix.

Now add most of the milk, slowly, and stir until combined. Keep the pan over a low heat and cover with a lid until the milk is absorbed and the seviyan is cooked completely. Check on it every couple of minutes, you may need to add more milk. Once cooked and soft, add the saffron, then pour the seviyan into a serving bowl and allow to cool.

Sprinkle with nuts and sultanas and decorate with silver leaf and/or rose petals. Refrigerate until ready to serve with ice-cold or warm milk or cream. Store in the fridge for up to a week, or in the freezer for months. It is great for breakfast.

Spiced and floral truffles

with dates, apricots, walnuts and pistachio

What keeps my daughter Ayaana grounded to her roots are the flavours of Pakistani cooking. I learnt much of my cooking by osmosis and it appears she is doing the same, which is why it wasn't a surprise when, at seven years old, she made up this recipe. Fun when made with little hands.

10g/¼ oz/scant 1½ tbsp walnuts

10g/¼ oz/scant 1½ tbsp unsalted pistachios

100g/3½ oz/⅔ cup soft dates, pitted

20g/¾ oz/scant ¼ cup soft dried apricots

30g/1 oz/2 tbsp butter, melted

1 cardamom pod, seeds removed and finely ground

1 tsp rose water

4 tbsp condensed milk

3 tbsp desiccated (dry unsweetened) coconut, finely ground

To decorate

2 tbsp dried pink rose petals

1 tbsp desiccated (dry unsweetened) coconut

1 tbsp finely ground pistachios

Preparation 20–25 minutes + 30 minutes chilling | **Makes** 6–8

Blitz the walnuts roughly in a food processor and set aside, then blitz the pistachios roughly and set aside separately.

Add all the main ingredients to a food processor with the ground nuts and blend until combined. Cover and chill in the fridge for 30 minutes.

When ready to make, take a heaped teaspoon of the cooled mixture and form it into a small ball, then roll it in a mix of rose petals, coconut and ground pistachios.

Serve immediately or store in an airtight container in the fridge for 1 week.

Milk fudge filo samosas

with coconut, cloves and pomegranate

I remember getting tiny crescent-shaped sweet parcels from friends celebrating Hindu festivals, and I always relished them. Traditionally these sweet samosas are called gujia, but here is my quick version using filo pastry and a filling made with homemade khoya (milk fudge), pomegranate seeds, desiccated coconut and poppy seeds.

130g/4 oz of filo
  (phyllo) pastry
150g/5½ oz khoya / milk
  fudge (see p23)
50g/1¾ oz desiccated (dry
  unsweetened) coconut,
  lightly toasted
1 tbsp poppy seeds, lightly
  dry-roasted
50g/1¾ oz/⅓ cup
  pomegranate seeds
1 tbsp blackcurrants
½ tsp ground cloves
a little ghee
about 100ml/3½ fl oz/scant
  ½ cup vegetable oil, for
  shallow-frying
whipped cream, to serve

Preparation 20 minutes | **Cooking** 15 minutes | **Makes** 8–9

Cut the filo pastry into 25cm/10-inch long x 5cm/2-inch wide strips and keep them covered under a damp tea towel so they don't dry out.

Mix all the remaining ingredients, up to and including the cloves, together in a bowl.

Begin to make the samosas by taking 2 filo sheets, brushing a little ghee on one side and sticking over the other. There is no need to grease the second sheet. Now with the narrow side facing you, add 1–2 teaspoons of the filling on one side, then begin to turn over to form a triangle. Keep repeating until you are left with a samosa-shaped pastry. Seal the end with a little ghee and repeat until all the filling and filo pastry is used up. Keep the samosas covered until ready to fry.

Heat the oil for shallow-frying in a frying pan and fry the samosas in batches for 3 minutes or so on each side until light brown and crispy. Remove with a slotted spoon and drain on kitchen paper. Keep warm in a foil pouch.

Serve hot with whipped cream.

Kashmiri shufta

Paneer cheese with floral spiced nuts

Dried fruits and paneer cheese are coated extravagantly with spiced rose sugar syrup, making this an irresistibly exotic Kashmiri festive offering. This is one of my favourite celebratory recipes.

7–8 dried dates, pitted and chopped into 4 pieces
2 tbsp ghee
100g/3½ oz firm paneer, cut into small squares
120g/4¼ oz/1 cup unsalted pistachios
60g/2¼ oz/½ cup walnuts
115g/4 oz/scant 1 cup blanched almonds
40g/1½ oz/⅓ cup pine nuts
80g/3 oz/⅔ cup cashews
50g/1¾ oz fresh coconut chunks
120g/4¼ oz/scant 1 cup sultanas (golden raisins)
400g/14 oz/2¼ cups golden caster (superfine) sugar
2 tbsp water

For the spices
4–5 cardamom pods, seeds removed and ground
½ tsp ground black pepper
½ tsp ground cinnamon
½ tsp ground nutmeg
½ tsp ground ginger
a large pinch of saffron threads
¼ tsp ground cloves
2–3 tbsp dried rose petals

Preparation 20 minutes + 20 minutes soaking | **Cooking** 20 minutes | **Serves** 6–8

Soak the chopped dates in a bowl of hot water for 20 minutes. Drain and place them on kitchen paper to soak up any excess water.

Heat 1 tablespoon of the ghee in a frying pan and fry the paneer until light golden brown on all sides. Remove from the pan and set aside.

Using the same pan, heat the remaining ghee and fry all the nuts, then fry the dried dates, coconut chunks and sultanas. Place them together with the fried paneer.

Heat the sugar and water together in another saucepan over a medium heat until the sugar dissolves. Once the sugar syrup begins to bubble, add all the spices and rose petals then add all the fried nuts, raisins and cheese.

Toss quickly to coat everything in the syrup and serve immediately.

Chilli mangoes
and ocean breeze
The sweetness of homecoming

The mesmerising orange dusk falling across the Arabian sea, and food stalls selling sweets and candy floss by the beach is an indelible Karachi memory.

Sizeable families bundled into vans travelling from afar for a Sunday night beach picnic, children screaming while rushing to the inviting water and their parents setting up the meal – each moment is relived as I stroll on that beach to this day. The silver sands blow that familiar gritty breeze through my hair and I think of family togetherness over food, fuelling a sense of belonging.

For me, living by the sea meant long walks on the beach lined with old wooden carts selling the forbidden pleasure gola ganda (shaved ice with sweet syrups), and breathing in the smells of spiced bhutta (corn on the cob) grilling on makeshift barbecues and the haunting wafts of seafood biryani that filled the air. My favourite snack, however, was the early summer kayri (raw mangoes), chopped and topped with a piquant mix of black salt and red chilli, leaving my senses heightened with each bite.

The simple combinations of Pakistani sweet snacks remind me of my homeland, where desserts don't just end a meal but rejoice in life, childhood and its innocence, no matter what your age. The flavours in this chapter are the ones that speak most of the comfort of homecoming.

Dadi's rasyawal pudding

Cane sugar molasses rice pudding

This recipe was always a favourite of my fathers when he was growing up. His mum originally made it with raw sugar cane juice and young rice (she called it 'naya chawwal' or 'new rice'). This is because traditionally this is a farmer's dish, made at the time when sugar and rice are harvested from the fields. Since fresh sugar cane juice isn't easy to find, I have substituted it (as do most people in my family) with a syrup made from jaggery (sugar cane molasses). If you can't find jaggery then use muscovado sugar instead.

100g/3½ oz/½ cup basmati rice
250g/9 oz/2 cups jaggery, grated or muscovado sugar
250–300ml/9–10 fl oz/ generous 1–1¼ cups water
Pakistani clotted cream / malai, to serve (see p23)

To decorate
2 tbsp thinly sliced fresh coconut
1 tbsp slivered pistachios
1 tbsp dried rose petals

Preparation 20 minutes + overnight soaking | **Cooking** 45–50 minutes | **Serves** 4–6

Rinse the rice, then allow it to soak in a bowl of water overnight. The next day, drain and set aside.

Place the jaggery in a heavy-based saucepan and pour in enough water to cover, then bring to the boil. As it boils, remove the scum that floats to the surface with a spoon and cook for 5–6 minutes until the jaggery has dissolved. Add the rice to the syrup and cook over a very low heat, stirring frequently and making sure that the rice doesn't stick to the base of the pan. Keep cooking until all the water is absorbed and rice is cooked though and shiny. You may need to add more water if the rice is still raw. Continue to cook until the water has been absorbed.

Decorate with coconut, pistachios and rose petals, then serve warm with malai clotted cream.

Dooth ki bottel

Rich milk and rose water drink with spice, seeds and nuts

Fresh milk from the farmer's shop is either delivered to your house each morning in a stainless-steel milk urn or bought from his farm shop. There was one treat that always enticed me to visit the milkman's shop – an empty fizzy drink bottle filled with an ice-cold full-cream buffalo's milk drink flavoured with a rich mix of pumpkin, poppy and sesame seeds, kewra and sugar. This recipe takes me right back to that indulgence.

600ml/20 fl oz/2½ cups
   whole milk
1 tbsp white poppy seeds
1 tbsp ground melon seeds
   or pumpkin seeds
½ tbsp sesame seeds
1 tbsp crushed pistachios
1 tbsp crushed blanched
   almonds
2–3 cardamom pods, seeds
   removed and finely
   crushed
1 tsp rose water or kewra
   (screwpine extract)
2–3 tsp brown sugar

Preparation 10 minutes | **Cooking** 15 minutes | **Serves** 5–6

Heat the milk, seeds, nuts, cardamom and rose water or kewra together in a heavy-based saucepan. Add the sugar and stir to dissolve.

Once the sugar has dissolved, bring to the boil, then turn the heat down and simmer for 5 minutes.

Chill in the fridge and drink cold.

Vimto gola ganda

Crushed ice topped with syrup

A summer day's excitement when I was growing up involved rickety wooden carts laden with bright syrups and brick-sized blocks of ice, shaded under jute bags. The ubiquitous gola ganda was a cool respite from the unforgiving Pakistani sun. I loved the combination of shaved ice, topped with rose, Vimto or ice-cream soda syrups, and the most delectable part was lashings of condensed milk and desiccated coconut. This is my version of this jaw-achingly sweet childhood snack.

15 ice cubes, crushed
2 tbsp condensed milk
2 tbsp rose syrup
2 tbsp vimto syrup
1 tbsp desiccated (dry
  unsweetened) coconut
  (can be dyed with gel food
  colour if desired)

Preparation 10 minutes | **Serves** 2–4

Place the crushed ice in a bowl and add the condensed milk and all the syrups.

If you would like to colour the coconut, add a drop of a gel-based food colour to the coconut and mix until the coconut turns a different colour.

Top the ice with the desiccated coconut and serve immediately.

Raw mango salad

with black salt, red chilli and lime

Just before Pakistani mango season, there would always be fruit stalls laden with small green raw mangoes. These sour fruits have a delicious taste when they are combined with complementary flavours. They can form the base for chutneys, jams and pickles, but I loved this simple snack of chopped raw mangoes spiced with a combination of red chilli, sea salt and a squeeze of lime or lemon.

....

2–3 raw mangoes, peeled
1 tsp red chilli powder
1 tsp Himalayan black salt
  (kalanamak)
½ tsp unrefined caster
  (superfine) sugar
juice of ½ lime

Preparation 10 minutes | **Serves** 2

Cut the mangoes into thin strips and discard the stones. Place the mango strips on a plate and add the red chilli flakes, salt, sugar and lemon or lime juice and toss together to combine.

Serve immediately.

Gulkand rose petal concentrate

Desi gulab are a local variety of oxblood roses that grow all year round in Pakistan. Adorning festival garlands and decadent desserts, these delicate petals are also used to make gulkand – a Pakistani rose petal jam with misri (rock sugar). My Nani (maternal grandmother) would pick roses from her garden, cook them slowly with misri, and we would then bottle them in an assortment of vintage glass jars. They were then left in the window to soak in the summer heat for a few weeks. Serve with pancakes or use as a filling in a plain Victoria sponge.

350ml/12 fl oz/1½ cups water (preferably filtered or spring)
55g/2 oz fresh rose petals (organic and pesticide free) or 40g/1½ oz dried rose petals
400g/14 oz/2 cups cane sugar
3 tbsp lemon juice
1 tsp fruit pectin

Preparation 15 minutes | **Cooking** 1 hour | **Makes** 1 × 300–400g/10½–14-oz jar

Place the water and rose petals in a heavy-based saucepan and bring to a gentle simmer for about 10 minutes.

Add half the sugar and allow it to dissolve, then add the lemon juice. This will enhance the colour of the petals. Simmer for another 10 minutes.

Now mix the remaining sugar and pectin together in a bowl. Then, 1 teaspoon at a time, slowly and gently stir the pectin syrup into the petal mixture. This should make sure that it doesn't clump together.

Simmer for another 15 minutes, stirring occasionally, until it is slightly thickened, but not as thick as jam since it sets once it is bottled.

Allow to cool slightly, then pour into a 300–400g/10½–14-oz sterilised jar (see p89) and leave to cool before sealing with a lid. Store in the fridge for 2 months. Use in cakes, pancakes, toast or rice pudding.

My cousins' mithai box

A shared treat of sweetened cottage cheese

My cousins (mother's brother's children) are half Bengali. Growing up I was close to them, and so many Bengali recipes have seeped into our kitchen, such as this mithai (sweetmeat), which is called sandesh. These treats are perfect for giving to friends and family, and this recipe is my gift to Sabrina, Natasha and Zain in memory of those carefree days in our grandmother's home together.

115g/4 oz/½ cup homemade curd cheese (see p56)

2 tbsp icing (confectioners') sugar, plus extra for dusting

4–5 cardamom pods, seeds removed and ground or 1 tsp rose water

To decorate

6 slivered or ground pistachios

6 pomegranate seeds

Preparation 20 minutes | **Cooking** 10–15 minutes | **Makes** 6

Place the homemade cheese, icing sugar and cardamom or rose water in a non-stick saucepan, mix well and cook over a low heat. The cheese will begin to melt and become softer. Continue cooking for about 10 minutes, or until it begins to form a ball and starts to leave the sides of the pan. Take off the heat and allow to cool.

Dust the work surface lightly with icing sugar. Knead the cooled dough, then roll a piece into a golf ball-sized ball and flatten it with your hands. Repeat until all the dough is used up.

Decorate each ball with pistachios or pomegranate seeds. Chill in the fridge and eat within a day.

Mummy's panjeri semolina granola

with mixed nuts, dried fruit and puffed Arabic gum

This is made with a mix of fortifying ingredients that are said to nurse ill health, energise new mothers, and provide a filling breakfast. Both my grandmothers and mother used to make this frequently, and each recipe was slightly different. This is my version using lots of dried berries, fruits and a variety of nuts. It is wonderful served with Greek yogurt, over cereal or even on its own.

2–3 tbsp ghee
2 tsp Arabic gum crystals
3–4 cardamom pods, seeds removed and ground
1 tbsp roughly chopped pistachios
1 tbsp roughly chopped almonds or pecans
1 tbsp roughly chopped walnuts
1 tbsp pumpkin seeds
1 tbsp raisins
2 tbsp chopped dried apricots
1 tbsp dried blueberries or cherries
1 tbsp dried cranberries
150g/5½ oz/scant 1 cup coarse semolina
1–2 tbsp thinly sliced fresh coconut
50g/1¾ oz/¼ cup caster (superfine) sugar

Preparation 15 minutes | **Cooking** 15 minutes | **Serves** 5–6

Heat 1 tablespoon of the ghee in a saucepan or frying pan over a medium heat. Carefully add the Arabic gum crystals and allow to puff up, about 1–2 minutes. Once puffed up, place on a piece of kitchen paper. Set aside.

Add the remaining ghee to the pan, reduce the heat to low, then toss in the cardamom, and all the nuts, seeds and dried fruit, and stir-fry for 3 minutes.

Add the semolina and fry for 5 minutes, mixing it in with all the nuts, fruit and coconut. Keep the heat on low and do not let the semolina burn on the base of the pan. The colour of the semolina should start to darken slightly.

Now add the sugar and fry, stirring constantly for 1 minute. Do not let the sugar dissolve.

Turn off the heat, allow the panjeri to cool, then serve or store in an airtight container for up to 3 days.

Pistachio chickie & Sesame rewri

Pistachio brittle & Sesame taffy

Winter dried fruit stalls heavily laden with pistachios, walnuts and pine nuts grown in the north of Pakistan would be the first sign of the changing weather. They were run mostly by Pathan men who had tiny fuel lamps that had smoke constantly billowing from them to attract the attention of passers-by (and of course keep the nuts warm). Along with nuts, they always had these two sweets, pistachio chickie (brittle) and sesame rewri (taffy), which were always very tempting.

For the pistachio chickie
1 tsp ghee, plus extra for greasing
200g/7 oz/1¼ cup jaggery, grated
2 tbsp water
250g/9 oz/2 cups unsalted pistachios
3–4 cardamom pods, seeds removed and ground
1 tbsp dried rose petals

For the sesame rewri
70g/2½ oz/½ cup sesame seeds
350ml/12 fl oz/1½ cups water
½ tsp salt
540g/1 lb 3 oz/3 cups caster (superfine) sugar
500g/1 lb 2 oz/1½ cups golden (light corn) syrup
3 tbsp ghee, plus extra for greasing
1 tbsp rose water

Preparation 25 minutes + 35 minutes | **Cooking** 20 minutes | **Serves** 5–6

For the pistachio chickie

Line a baking tray with greaseproof paper and grease with butter or ghee. Combine the grated jaggery and water in a heavy-based saucepan and bring to the boil. Bring the temperature to 127°C (260°F) on a sugar thermometer. Add the nuts and ghee and heat to 143°C (289°F).

Add the cardamom and rose petals to the nuts and jaggery just before taking off the heat. Stir quickly and pour on to the prepared baking tray. Using a wooden spoon, spread and flatten the mixture to 5mm/¼ inch thick. Allow to dry. Cut into squares and store in an airtight container for 1 week.

For the sesame rewri

Line a baking tray with greaseproof paper. Dry-roast the sesame seeds in a dry frying pan, then spread out on the prepared baking tray and cool. Put the water, salt, sugar and golden syrup in a heavy-based saucepan and heat over a medium heat. Do not stir and heat until the mixture reaches triple thread stage 127°C (260°F) on a sugar thermometer (see p22). Add the ghee and rose water, then turn off the heat, leaving the thermometer in the pan and cool to 66°C (150°F).

Rub ghee on your hands and, picking up 3 tablespoons of the mixture at a time, pull and fold the mixture repeatedly until it turns a creamy white. Taking a 10cm/4-inch long piece, pull the candy until it is 5mm/¼ inch thick, then cut into 1cm/½-inch pieces, toss in the roasted sesame seeds and place on a sheet of greaseproof paper to dry.

Karachi halva

with pumpkin seeds and cashews

This Turkish delight-like sweet was invented in my home town. As a child I would pass by mithai (sweetmeat) shops and look longingly at the many vibrant, colourful sweets on offer. There was one sweet that always caught my eye – orange, green or pink chewy, rubber-like shiny halva cut into neat squares and topped with nuts and pumpkin seeds. Magical.

50g/1¾ oz/½ cup cornflour (cornstarch)

590ml/20 fl oz/2½ cups water

¼ tsp pink gel food colour

2 tbsp ghee, plus extra for greasing

1½ tbsp chopped cashews

1 tbsp pumpkin seeds

300g/10½ oz/1½ cups caster (superfine) sugar

3–4 cardamom pods, seeds removed and ground

To decorate

1 tbsp dried rose petals

1 tbsp slivered pistachios

1 tbsp raisins

Preparation 20 minutes + 1 hour cooling | **Cooking** 30–40 minutes | **Makes** 6–10

Place the cornflour in a bowl, add 350ml/12 fl oz/1½ cups water and mix until smooth. Add the food colour, stir and mix well, then set aside.

Grease a large plate with ghee and set aside.

Heat 1 tablespoon of the ghee in a wok-style pan over a medium heat, add the cashews and pumpkin seeds and roast for 30 seconds, or until golden brown. Set aside.

In the same pan, add the sugar and 240ml/8 fl oz/1 cup water and heat over a medium heat to allow the sugar to dissolve. Slowly add the cornflour mixture, stirring constantly.

Now turn the heat down very low and keep stirring, the mixture will start turning glossy and coming together. It will thicken slowly, but don't stop stirring otherwise lumps will form.

Now add the remaining ghee and the ground cardamom and mix well. The mixture should be very thick by now. When the halva starts to leave the sides of the pan and becomes very shiny, add the roasted nuts and seeds. Turn off the heat and stir. The ghee should start coming to the surface. Transfer the mixture to the greased plate and level it with the back of a spoon.

Allow to cool for at least 1 hour before cutting it into squares and decorating with rose petals, pistachios and raisins.

Makhan roti cheeni

Chappatis rubbed with homemade butter and raw sugar

Sometimes the best treats are those made with love and leftovers. This is a simple combination of chappati topped with homemade butter and raw cane sugar, something my Nani (maternal grandmother) and my mother would give me as a snack or just because leftover bread needed eating. The comfort of those flavours still take me back to my childhood, I know my daughter Ayaana will come to love this as well, keeping my Pakistani heritage alive as she grows up in Scotland.

For the chappatis
135g/4¾ oz/scant 1 cup wholemeal (wholewheat) flour, plus extra for dusting
a pinch of salt
200ml/7 fl oz/scant 1 cup water

For the makhan
150ml/5 fl oz/⅔ cup thick double (heavy) cream
10–12 ice cubes
very cold water, as needed
a pinch of salt

2 tbsp raw cane sugar or caster (superfine) sugar

Preparation 30 minutes | **Cooking** 25 minutes | **Makes** 6–8

Begin by making the chappati dough. Mix the flour and salt together with enough of the water as needed to make a soft dough. Cover the dough with a damp tea towel and set aside at room temperature.

To make the makhan, put the cream and ice in a blender, add water, a little at a time, and blend until the cream starts to separate and you start to get butter floating to the top. Stop blending and collect the butter in a muslin cloth. Squeeze out all the liquid and set the butter aside on a plate in the fridge.

Now make the chappatis. Flour a clean work surface. Taking tennis ball-sized pieces of the dough, roll them out into round flatbreads with a rolling pin, until they are about 5mm/¼ inch thick.

Heat a flat pancake pan or tawa over a medium heat. Place each chappati on the hot pan and press down using a tea towel from the corners, until the base is light brown, about 1 minute. Flip over and cook on the other side for 1–2 minutes, then remove from the pan and place in a foil pouch to keep warm.

To assemble, place a hot chappati on a plate, rub with the makhan and sprinkle with raw sugar, then roll up and eat immediately.

Acknowledgements

This second book was just as challenging as my first, *Summers Under the Tamarind Tree*, if not more so. It has been a journey through the sweet flavours of my homeland and some of my fondest memories of growing up, and sharing them feels like an offering to everyone who reads it.

This book would not have been achievable without the belief, dedication and commitment of many people. So I'd like to thank:

My commissioning editor Zena Alkayat, who has turned my basic idea into a thing of beauty.

Sarah Allberrey, for the beautiful design that echoes the sentiment and story of my first book, but gives it its own identity.

Joanna Blythman and Felicity Cloake, for their constant support, time and kind words.

My parents, for teaching me what it means to share happiness, joy and sadness in equal measure. To my mother, for instilling perfection, and to my daughter Ayaana, for being a reason to keep cooking.

My wonderful grandmothers, who may be long gone, but whose recipes still bring joy to my life.

And a very special thanks to Graeme Taylor, who has always helped me find the words that get garbled in my confused head, and who has always nudged me to keep going.

Further thanks go to my literary agent Claudia Young (Greene & Heaton) for her support and faith. Joanna Yee for stunning photos (as always), Alexander Breeze for prop styling, Kathy Steer for recipe editing, Sarah Chatwin for proofreading and Marianne Ryan for indexing. Finally to Kausar Usmani, Moneeza Khan, Nuzhat Usmani, Fauzia Usmani Saeed and Gulnaz for their invaluable help with recipes.

All travel photography © Getty Images

p2 A Shahi Qila fresco painting with a figurative floral motive in Lahore (myloupe); p6 A Kalash woman dries apricots on the roof of her house in Anish Villlage, Bumburet (Eric Chretien); p8 (top) The mountains of Gilgit-Baltistan (Zahid Ali Khan); p8 (bottom) A passenger on board one of Karachi's colourful mini buses (Asif Hassan/AFP); p11 A street stall in Islamabad with traditional Pakistani sweets including pakora, jalebi and samosas (Metin Aktas/Anadolu Agency); p12 (top) Labourers load sugar canes onto horse-drawn carts at a fruit and vegetable market in Lahore (Arif Ali/AFP); p12 (bottom) A vendor sells fruit in Karachi (Bashir Osman). p28 (top) A farmer picks dates from a tree (Raja Islam); p28 (bottom) Fruit sellers at a market in Lahore (Gavin Quirke); p50 (top) A cattle farmer herds buffalo(Amir Mukhtar); p50 (bottom) A street seller prepares fresh samosas (Raja Islam); p72 (top) Children fly kites on the outskirts of Islamabad (Farooq Naeem); p72 (bottom) A bubbling pan of gulab jamun (Paul Harris); p94 The Hunza Valley in the Gilgit-Baltistan region of Pakistan (Yasir Nisar); p116 (top) Baskets filled with saffron flowers in a field in Jammu and Kashmir (Dinodia Photo); p116 (bottom) Spices for sale at market (Donald Iain Smith); p138 A rose-petal vendor in Multan (Christophe Boisvieux); p160 The end of the day on Karachi beach (thecolourbox).

Index

A

Afghani gosh-e-fil (elephant ear-shaped fried pastry with ground pistachio) 118

Afghani asabia el aroos (pine nut, pistachio and almond filled filo pastry soaked in rose water syrup) 120

Afghani awb-e-dundawn (rose water biscuits) 136

almonds 24

    Afghani asabia el aroos (filo pastry) 120

    almond oil 39

    badam ki jali (marzipan lace) 52

    badami kulcha (meringues) 123

    badami zafran halva ladoo (almond and saffron balls) 135

    dar ni puri (sweet puris with filling) 65

    ground almonds 123, 135

    Kashmiri shufta (paneer cheese with spiced nuts) 159

    Mummy's panjeri semolina granola 175

    sohan saffron honey caramels 77

    sugar almonds 51

almond milk: sharbat (buckwheat porridge) 32

    sweet vermicelli pudding 36

apple: apple halva with cardamom and pomegranate 102

    spiced apple samosas 96

apricots, Hunza: chamborogh (apricots stewed with cream) 100

    fresh curd burutz cheese 111

    khubani ka meetha (apricots with cream and custard) 51

    mulberry and cherry fruit leather 105

    Mummy's panjeri semolina granola 175

    sharbat (buckwheat porridge with stewed apricots) 32

    spiced and floral truffles 155

apricot oil: Hunza barove giyaling (buckwheat pancakes with summer berries) 39

B

badam ki jali (cardamom and rose water marzipan lace) 52

badami kulcha (almond and cardamom meringues) 123

badami zafran halva ladoo (ground almond and saffron balls) 135

bakar khani (sweet puff pastry biscuits) 46

baklava: Afghani asabia el aroos (filled filo pastries) 120

balushahi (festive glazed curd doughnut) 142

barfi ('heart' mithai) 17

bejewelled Parsi wedding custard 60

berries: bramble gulgulay (blackberry doughnuts) 45

    Hunza barove giyaling (buckwheat pancakes) 39

    mulberry and blackberry stew 106

biscuits: Afghani awb-e-dundawn (rose water biscuits) 136

    badarmi kulcha (almond and cardamom meringue) 123

    bakar khani (sweet puff pastry biscuits) 46

    nan-e nokhochi (chickpea flour shortbread) 130

blackberries: bramble gulgulay (blackberry doughnuts) 45

    mulberry and blackberry stew 106

bramble gulgulay (blackberry doughnuts) 45

bread: pakwan (wheat flour and jaggery rolls) 112

    pudding: shahi tukra brioche bread pudding 144

    sweet: dar ni puri (sweet puris with filling) 65

    tandoori 73

breakfasts 29, 31, 36–9, 46, 49, 73, 78, 153, 175

brioche: shahi tukra brioche bread pudding 144

buckwheat 23: Hunza barove giyaling (buckwheat pancakes with summer berries) 39

    semolina halva ladoos 87

    sharbat (buckwheat porridge with stewed apricots) 32

buffalo milk 10, 19, 51, 68, 74, 133, 165

burutz (lassi-based cheese) 24

    fresh curd burutz cheese 111

butter, homemade: makhan roti cheeni (chappatis) 181

C

caramels: sohan saffron honey caramels 77

cardamom 10, 17, 22, 73, 139

    Afghani gosh-e-fil (elephant-ear fried pastries) 118

    Afghani awb-e-dundawn (rose water biscuits) 136

    apple halva with pomegranate 102

    badam ki jali (rose water marzipan lace) 52

    badami kulcha (almond meringues) 123

    balushahi (festive glazed curd doughnuts) 142

    bramble gulgulay (blackberry doughnuts) 45

    dooth ki bottel 165

    gajar ka halva (carrot halva) 141

    gajrela (carrot rice pudding) 54

    Karachi halva with cashews 179

    pistachio chickie & sesame rewri (brittle & taffy) 176

    khanfaroush (spiced crumpets) 126

    Lahori kheer rice pudding 74

    malpura semolina pancakes 84

    mango, cardamom, saffron and red chilli murraba (preserve) 89

    memon lappi (crunchy oats with jaggery) 71

    nan-e nokhochi (chickpea flour shortbread) 130

    pakwan (wheat flour and jaggery rolls) 112

    pomegranate, rose and cardamom halva jelly 109

    rabri kulfi sticks with honey and bay leaf 63

    rose lab-e-shireen (Pakistani trifle) 147

    rice flour pancakes with black cardamom 83

roasted nuts and rock sugar 67
saffron and cashew bal mithai (sweets) 129
saffron-infused zarda (sweet rice) 150
sesame gajak 124
shahi tukra brioche bread pudding 144
shakarkandi ki kheer (sweet potato pudding) 90
shakarpara (sweet pastry puffs) 40
sharbat (buckwheat porridge with stewed apricots) 32
spiced apple samosas 96
sweet parathas with filling 43
sweet vermicelli pudding 36
whipped semolina halva 31
carrot: gajar ka halva 17, 141
    gajar mukhadi (semolina and carrot pudding) 115
    gajrela (carrot rice pudding) 54
cashews: Karachi halva with pumpkin seeds and cashews 179
    Kashmiri shufta (paneer cheese with nuts) 159
    saffron and cashew bal mithai (sweets) 129
chaat: pakwan (wheat flour and jaggery rolls) 112
chaat masala: spiced fruit chaat with guava, pomegranate and mango 34
chamborogh (stewed Hunza apricots with cream and
    apricot kernels) 100
channa daal 23: dar ni puri (sweet puris with filling) 65
cheese 24
    fresh curd burutz cheese 111
    Kashmiri shufta (paneer cheese with nuts) 159
    kishmish paneer (fresh curd cheese) 56
    my cousins' mithai box (sweet cottage cheese) 172
    Rabri kulfi sticks (ice cream) 63
cherries 36
    candied: dar ni puri (sweet puris with filling) 65
    Hunza barove giyaling (buckwheat pancakes) 39
    mulberry and blackberry stew 106
    mulberry and cherry fruit leather 105
    roasted nuts and rock sugar 67
chickpea flour (mootichoor) 23, 87
    nan-e nokhochi (shortbread) 130
    Pakistani jalebis (fermented doughnuts) 78
    roasted nuts and rock sugar 67
chillies: kayri (mangoes with black salt and red chilli) 161
    mango, cardamom, saffron and red chilli murraba 89
    spiced fruit chaat (fruit salad) 34
Chitrali rishiki (pancakes with mulberry syrup) 99
cinnamon: Lahori kheer rice pudding 74
    memon lappi (crunchy oats) 71
    pakwan (wheat flour and jaggery rolls) 112
cloves 22, 139

gajar ka halva (carrot halva) 141
nan-e nokhochi (chickpea flour shortbread) 130
qawwami seviyan (vermicelli dessert) 153
saffron-infused zarda (sweet rice) 150
coconut 135
    gajar ka halva (carrot halva) 141
    Kashmiri shufta (paneer cheese) 159
    milk fudge filo samosas 156
    Mummy's panjeri semolina granola 75
    roasted nuts and rock sugar 67
    semolina halva ladoos 87
    spiced and floral truffles 155
    sweet parathas 43
    whipped semolina halva 31
coconut milk: rice flour pancakes 83
    rose and lychee sagodanna pudding 49
condensed milk 21
cream, clotted (malai) 23–4:
    mango, thyme and pink salt 68
crumpets: khanfaroush (spiced crumpets) 126
curd cheese 24
    fresh curd burutz cheese 111
    kishmish paneer (with raisins and sultanas) 56
    my cousins' mithai box 172
custard: bejewelled Parsi wedding custard 60
    dahi ki kheer (baked saffron yogurt) 93

D

Dadi's rasyawal pudding (cane sugar molasses rice pudding) 162
dahi ki kheer (baked saffron yogurt) 93
dar ni puri (sweet puris filled with lentils, mace, raisins and candied
    cherries) 65
dates: roasted nuts and rock sugar 67
    spiced apple samosas 96
    spiced and floral truffles 155
    sweet parathas 43
dawwat (feast) 13, 139
dooth ki bottel (milk and rose water drink with spice, seeds and nuts) 165
doothpati (cardamom and milk tea) 40
doughnuts: balushahi (festive glazed curd doughnut) 142
    bramble gulgulay (blackberry doughnuts) 45
    Pakistani jalebis (fermented, in syrup) 78
drinks: dooth ki bottel (milk and rose water drink) 165
    see also tea

F

falooda 73
    Lahori falooda (kulfi float) 78
falsa berries 29
fennel seeds: memon lappi (crunchy oats) 71
figs: fresh curd burutz cheese 111
    Lahori kheer rice pudding 74
filo pastry: Afghani asabia el aroos (filled filo pastries) 120
    milk fudge filo samosas 156
firni (ground rice) 59, 73
fruit 29, 95, 139
    fresh curd burutz cheese 111
    spiced fruit chaat (fruit salad) 34
    see also apricot, apple, cherry, blackberry, cranberry, mulberry, pear, plum, pomegranate, raspberry
fruit, dried 36, 100, 105, 106, 111, 148, 150, 159, 175, 176

G

gajar ka halva (carrot halva served with whipped cream) 141
gajar mukhadi (semolina and carrot pudding) 115
gajrela (carrot rice pudding) 54
ghee 24
ginger 22
    mulberry and blackberry stew 106
gola ganda (shaved ice with syrups) 161
    Vimto gola ganda (crushed ice topped with syrup) 166
gosh-e-fil (elephant ears) 118
granola: Mummy's panjeri semolina granola 175
    roasted nuts and rock sugar 67
ground rice (firni) 59, 73
guava: spiced fruit chaat with pomegranate and mango 34
gujia (sweet samosas): milk fudge filo samosas 156
gulgulay: bramble gulgulay (blackberry doughnuts) 45
gulkand rose petal concentrate 171
gur (sugar) 21

H

halva 73, 77, 139
    apple halva 102
    badami zafran halva ladoo (almond balls) 135
    gajar mukhadi (semolina and carrot pudding) 115
    Karachi halva 179
    multani sohan (sprouted wheat halva) 77
    pomegranate, rose and cardamom halva jelly 109
    semolina halva ladoos 87
    whipped semolina halva 31
hazelnuts: roasted nuts and rock sugar 67
honey 22
    mulberry and blackberry stew 106
    rabri kulfi sticks 63
    sohan saffron honey caramels 77
Hunza barove giyaling (buckwheat pancakes with summer berries, walnuts and apricot oil) 39

I

ice cream: Lahori falooda 80
    Peshawari pistachio ice cream 133
    rabri kulfi sticks 63
ice: vimto gola golanda (crushed ice topped with syrup) 166

J

jaggery (sugar) 21
    bramble gulgulay (blackberry doughnuts) 45
    Dadis rasyawal pudding 162
    pistachio chickie & sesame rewri (brittle & taffy) 176
    malida (wheat and jaggery dessert) 51
    mango, thyme and pink salt 68
    memon lappi (crunchy oats) 71
    pakwan (wheat flour and jaggery rolls) 112
    rice flour pancakes 83
    roasted nuts and rock sugar 67
    sesame gajak 124
jalebis 73
    Pakistani jalebis (fermented doughnuts) 78
jam: gulkand rose petal concentrate 171
jelly: rose lab-e-shireen (Pakistani trifle) 147

K

Karachi halva with pumpkin seeds and cashews 179
Kashmiri phirin (ground rice pudding with saffron) 59
Kashmiri shufta (paneer cheese with floral spiced nuts) 159
kewra (screwpine extract) 23, 139
    dooth ki bottel (milk and rose water drink) 165
    pistachio chickie & sesame rewri (brittle & taffy) 176
    Lahori kheer rice pudding 74
    Peshawari pistachio ice cream 133
    pomegranate, rose and cardamom halva jelly 109
khanfaroush (spiced saffron crumpets with honey) 126
kheer (dessert) 59
    Dahi ki kheer (baked saffron yogurt) 93
    shakarkandi ki kheer (sweet potato pudding) 90
    slow-cooked Lahori kheer rice pudding 74

khoya (milk fudge) 17, 23
    badami zafran halva ladoo (almond balls) 135
    gajar mukhadi (semolina and carrot pudding) 115
    milk fudge filo samosas 156
    saffron and cashew bal mithai (sweets) 129
    sweet parathas 43
khubani ka meetha (apricots with cream and custard) 51
kishmish paneer (fresh curd cheese with raisins and sultanas) 56
kuch (homemade butter) 24
kulfi: Lahori falooda (with glass noodles and syrup) 78
    rabri (milk solids): rabri kulfi sticks 63

L

ladoos: badami zafran halva ladoo (almond balls) 135
    semolina halva ladoos 87
Lahori falooda (kulfi float with basil seeds, glass noodles and
    rose syrup) 78
Lahori kheer (slow cooked rice pudding with black cumin and
    pine nuts) 74
lentils: dar ni puri (sweet puris with filling) 65
lychees: rose and lychee sagodanna pudding 49
    rose lab-e-shireen (Pakistani trifle) 147

M

mace 23
    dar ni puri (sweet puris with filling) 65
makhan (homemade butter) 24
    makhan roti cheeni (chappatis with raw sugar) 181
malai (clotted cream) 23
    Dadi's rasyawal pudding 162
    mango, thyme and pink salt 68
malida (wheat and jaggery dessert) 51
malpura semolina pancakes 84
mangoes 161
    mango, cardamom, saffron and red chilli murraba 89
    mango, thyme and pink salt with rose water malai 68
    raw mango salad 168
    rose lab-e-shireen (Pakistani trifle) 147
    spiced fruit chaat with guava and pomegranate 34
marzipan: badam ki jali (cardamom and rose water lace) 52
memon lappi (crunchy oats with jaggery, cinnamon and fennel seeds) 71
meva naan (sweet bread with dried fruit) 148
milk 22, 24, 139
    dooth ki bottel (milk and rose water drink) 165
    fudge see khoya
    milk fudge filo samosas 156
milk puddings 63

    bejewelled Parsi wedding custard 60
    dahi ki kheer (baked saffron yogurt) 93
    gajrela (carrot rice pudding) 54
    Kashmiri phirin (ground rice pudding with saffron) 59
    Lahori kheer (rice pudding) 74
    qawwami seviyan (vermicelli dessert) 153
    shahi tukra brioche bread pudding 144
    shakarkandi ki kheer (sweet potato pudding) 90
    rose and lychee sagodanna pudding 49
    sweet vermicelli pudding 36
milk, buffalo 51, 74
misri (rock sugar) 21, 67, 68, 171
mithai 13, 17, 73, 135, 139, 142, 172, 179
    badami zafran halva ladoo 135
    Karachi halva with pumpkin seeds and cashews 179
    saffron and cashew bal mithai 129
    semolina halva ladoos 87
moong daal 23, 87
mootichoor (chickpea flour) 87
mulberries 95, 105
    Chitrali rishiki (pancakes with mulberry syrup) 99
    mulberry and blackberry stew 106
    mulberry and cherry fruit leather with crushed walnuts and
      pistachios 105
multani sohan (sprouted wheat halva) 77
Mummy's panjeri semolina granola with mixed nuts, dried fruit and
    puffed Arabic gum 175
my cousins' mithai box 172

N

namakpara (salty pastry snack) 40
nan-e nokhochi (chickpea flour shortbread with cloves) 130
nankhatai (spiced semolina shortbread) 51
noodles, glass: Lahori falooda 78
nutmeg 23
nuts 24
    Mummy's panjeri semolina granola with mixed nuts, dried fruit and
      puffed Arabic gum 175
    see also almonds, pecans, pine nuts, pistachios, walnuts

O

oats: memon lappi 71
oil, vegetable 24

P

Pakistan 9–13
Pakistani jalebis (spiralled fermented doughnuts in
        turmeric-infused syrup) 78
pakwan (wheat and jaggery rolls with aniseed) 112
pancakes: Chitrali rishiki (pancakes with mulberry syrup) 99
        Hunza barove giyaling (with summer berries) 39
        malpura semolina pancakes 84
        rice flour pancakes 83
paneer cheese: kashmiri shufta (paneer with spiced nuts) 159
parathas: sweet parathas with filling 43
pastries: Afghani gosh-e-fil (fried pastries) 118
        Afghani asabia el aroos (filled filo pastries) 120
        bakar khani (sweet puff pastry biscuits) 46
        filo pastry 120, 156
        milk fudge filo samosas 156
        namakpara (salty pastry snack) 40
        puris 65
        shakarpara (sweet pastry puffs) 40
pecans: Mummy's panjeri semolina granola 175
pepper, black 22
Peshawari pistachio ice cream 133
pine nuts 24
        Afghani asabia el aroos (filled filo pastries) 120
        dar ni puri (sweet bread with filling) 65
        Kashmiri shufta (paneer with spiced nuts) 159
        Lahori khee (rice pudding) 74
        semolina halva ladoos with buckwheat 87
pistachios 24
        Afghani asabia el aroos (filled filo pastries) 120
        Afghani gosh-e-fil (fried pastries) 118
        bramble gulgulay (blackberry doughnuts) 45
        chickie (sweet sesame brittle) 176
        gajar ka halva (carrot halva) 141
        mulberry and cherry fruit leather 105
        Mummy's panjeri semolina granola 175
        Peshawari pistachio ice cream 133
        saffron-infused zarda (sweet rice) 150
        spiced and floral truffles 155
pomegranate: apple halva with cardamom and pomegranate 102
        milk fudge filo samosas 156
        pomegranate, rose and cardamom halva jelly 109
        spiced fruit chaat with guava and mango 34
        whipped semolina halva 31

porridge: memon lappi (crunchy oats) 71
        sharbat (buckwheat porridge with apricots) 32
        sweet vermicelli pudding 36
preserve: mango, cardamom, saffron and chilli murraba 89
puddings: Dadi's rasyawal pudding 162
        rose and lychee sagodanna pudding 49
        shahi tukra brioche bread pudding 144
        sweet vermicelli pudding 36
        see also milk puddings
puff pastry: bakar khani (sweet puff pastry biscuits) 46
pumpkin seeds Karachi halva 179
puris 73
        dar ni puri (sweet puris with filling) 65

Q

qawwami seviyan (roasted vermicelli topped with nuts) 153

R

rabri (milk solids): rabri kulfi sticks with honey, cardamom and bay leaf 63
raisins: dar ni puri (sweet puris with filling) 65
        kishmish paneer (fresh curd cheese with raisins and sultanas) 56
raspberries: malpura semolina pancakes 84
        whipped semolina halva with raspberry sauce 31
rasyawal pudding: Dadi's rasyawal pudding 162
rice 23
        Dadi's rasyawal pudding 162
        gajrela (carrot rice pudding) 54
        Kashmiri phirin (ground rice pudding with saffron) 59
        Lahori kheer (rice pudding with black cumin and pine nuts) 74
        rice flour pancakes with black cardamom and poppy seeds 83
        saffron-infused zarda (sweet rice) 150
        shakarkandi ki kheer (sweet potato pudding) 90
ricotta 23: rabri kulfi sticks with honey and cardamom 63
        shahi tukra brioche (bread pudding) 144
roasted nuts and rock sugar with hazelnuts, dates, dried cherries and
        chickpea flour 67
rock sugar see misri
rose lab-e-shireen (Pakistani trifle with lychee, mango, cardamom,
        milk and vermicelli) 147
rose 23, 117, 139
        gulkand rose petal concentrate 171
        Kashmiri phirin (ground rice pudding with saffron) 59
        Lahori falooda (kulfi float) 78
        pomegranate, rose and cardamom halva jelly 109
        rose and lychee sagodanna pudding 49
        rose lab-e-shireen (Pakistani trifle) 147

rose water badam ki jali (cardamom marzipan lace) 52
    Afghani asabia el aroos (filled filo pastries) 120
    Afghani awb-e-dundawn (rose water biscuits) 136
    dooth ki bottel (milk and rose water drink) 165
    gajar ka halva (carrot halva) 141

S

saffron 10, 22, 117, 139, 142
    badami zafran halva ladoo (almond balls) 135
    dahi ki kheer (baked saffron yogurt) 93
    gajar ka halva (carrot halva) 141
    Kashmiri phirin (ground rice pudding with saffron) 59
    khanfaroush (spiced crumpets) 126
    mango, cardamom, saffron and chilli murraba 89
    Pakistani jalebis (fermented doughnuts) 78
    qawwami seviyan (vermicelli dessert) 153
    saffron and cashew bal mithai (caramelised sweets with
        sugar nibs) 129
    saffron-infused zarda (sweet rice with nuts, coconut,
        candied fruit and khoya) 150
    shahi tukra brioche bread pudding 144
    sohan saffron honey caramels 77
sago: rose and lychee sagodanna pudding 49
    sagodanna: rose and lychee sagodanna pudding 49
samosas 73
    milk fudge filo samosas with coconut, cloves and pomegranate 156
    spiced apple samosas 96
sandesh (mithai) 172
screwpine see kewra
semolina 23:
    gajar mukhadi (semolina and carrot pudding) 115
    malpura semolina pancakes 84
    Mummy's panjeri semolina granola 175
    semolina halva ladoos with buckwheat groats, pine nuts,
        aniseed and coconut 87
    spiced apple samosas 96
    whipped semolina halva 31
sesame
    bakar khani (sweet puff pastry biscuits) 46
    pistachio chickie & sesame rewri (brittle & taffy) 176
    sesame gajak (sesame seed and jaggery melt-in-the-mouth snaps) 124
seviyan (vermicelli): qawwami seviyan 153
shahi tukra brioche bread pudding with saffron, ricotta, cranberries
    and chopped nuts 144
shakar (sugar) 21, see also jaggery
shakarkandi ki kheer (sweet potato pudding) 90
shakarpara (sweet pastry puffs) 40

shakarpostik (fruit leather) 105
sharbat (buckwheat porridge with pink salt, cardamom and stewed
    Hunza apricots) 32
sheer khurma (saffron-infused drink) 139
shirni (mulberry syrup) 22:
    Chitrali rishiki (pancakes) 99
shortbread: nan-e nokhochi (with chickpea flour) 130
sohan saffron honey caramels with rose water, pistachio and almonds 77
spiced and floral truffles with dates, apricots, walnuts and pistachio 155
spiced apple samosas 96
spiced fruit chaat with guava, pomegranate and mango 34
sugar 21, see also jaggery and sugar syrups
sugar almonds 51
syrups 21, 40, 49, 71, 78, 84, 102, 120, 124, 142, 153, 159, 162
sweet parathas filled with date, walnut and milk fudge 43
sweet potato: shakarkandi ki kheer 90
sweet vermicelli pudding with black cardamom and vanilla 36

T

tapioca: rose and lychee sagodanna pudding 49
tea: 29, 39, 43, 73, 95, 112
thyme: mango, thyme and pink salt 68
toffee: sohan saffron honey caramels 77

V

vermicelli 23
    qawwami seviyan (vermicelli dessert) 153
    rose lab-e-shireen (Pakistani trifle) 147
    sweet vermicelli pudding 36
vimto gola golanda (crushed ice topped with syrup) 166

W

walnuts 24
    gajar mukhadi (semolina and carrot pudding) 115
    mulberry and cherry fruit leather 105
    Mummy's panjeri semolina granola 175
    spiced and floral truffles 155
    sweet parathas with filling 43
whipped semolina halva 31

Y

yogurt 24
    balushahi (festive glazed curd doughnut) 142
    dahi ki kheer (baked saffron yogurt) 93
    fresh curd burutz cheese 111
    meva naan (sweet bread with dried fruit) 148
    Pakistani jalebis (fermented doughnuts) 78